STUDIES IN THE HISTORY

OF THE

ROMAN PROVINCE

OF SYRIA

I０２１１２１０

A DISSERTATION

PRESENTED TO THE

FACULTY OF PRINCETON UNIVERSITY
IN CANDIDACY FOR THE DEGREE
OF DOCTOR OF PHILOSOPHY

BY

GUSTAVE ADOLPHUS HARRER

Wipf & Stock
PUBLISHERS
Eugene, Oregon

Wipf and Stock Publishers
199 W 8th Ave, Suite 3
Eugene, OR 97401

Studies in the History of the Roman Province of Syria
By Harrer, Gustave Adolphus
ISBN: 1-59752-463-8
Publication date 2/16/2006
Previously published by Princeton University Press, 1915

PREFACE

The general topic of this thesis was suggested to me by Professor David Magie, Jr., to whom I am further greatly indebted for constant helpful advice and criticism throughout the preparation of it. I wish to express my thanks to Professor Duane Reed Stuart who has read the thesis in manuscript, and has given me many valuable suggestions. To Professor William K. Prentice I am also under obligations for advice. I would like to acknowledge my gratitude to all my instructors in Princeton during my graduate and undergraduate years.

GUSTAVE A. HARRER.

Princeton University
March 27, 1915

ABBREVIATIONS

A. A. E. S. III = W. K. Prentice, Greek and Latin Inscriptions. Part III of the Publications of an American Archaeological Expedition to Syria in 1899-1900. N. Y., 1908.

A. E. = L'Année épigraphique.

A. E. M. = Archaeologisch-epigraphische Mitteilungen aus Oester-reich-Ungarn.

A. J. A. = American Journal of Archaeology.

A. J. Ph. = American Journal of Philology.

Abh. d. Akad. zu Berlin = Abhandlungen der Königlichen Akademie der Wissenschaften zu Berlin.

Abh. Sächs. Ges. d. Wiss. = Abhandlungen der Königlichen Sächsischen Gesellschaft der Wissenschaften, Leipzig.

B. A. R. = Bolletino dell' Assoc. Archaeologica romana.

B. C. H. = Bulletin de Correspondence hellénique.

B. G. U. = Griechische Urkunden aus dem Königlichen Museum zu Berlin.

B. J. = Bonner Jahrbücher.

B. M. C. = British Museum Catalogue of Greek Coins. London 1873—

B. M. Gk. Pap. = Greek Papyri in the British Museum. Edited by F. G. Kenyon. London.

B. S. N. A. = Bulletin de la Société national des Antiquaires de France.

Babelon, Rois = E. C. F. Babelon, Les Rois de Syrie, d'Arménie, et de Commagène. Paris, 1890.

Brit. Sch. Ath. = British School at Athens. Annual.

Brünnow, Arabia = R. E. Brünnow und A. von Domaszewski, Die Provincia Arabia. Strassburg 1904-1909.

Bull. dell Inst. = Bulletino dell' Instituto di Corrispondenza Archeo-logica.

C. I. G. = Corpus Inscriptionum Graecarum.

C. I. L. = Corpus Inscriptionum Latinarum.

Chapot, Front. Euphart. = Victor Chapot, La Frontière de l'Euphrate de Pompée à la conquête arabe. Paris, 1907.

Chapot, Prov. Asie = Victor Chapot, La Province romaine procon-sulaire d'Asie. Paris, 1904.

Cohen = H. Cohen, Médailles Impériales. Paris, 1880-1890.

Dessau = H. Dessau, Inscriptiones Latinae Selectae. Berlin, 1892—.

5

Dittenberger, Or. Gr. Inscr. = W. Dittenberger, Orientis Graeci Inscriptiones Selectae. Leipzig, 1903-1905.

Domaszewski, G. R. K. = A. von Domaszewski, Geschichte der Römischen Kaiser. Leipzig, 1909.

Domaszewski, Rangord. = A. von Domaszewski, Die Rangordnung des Römischen Heeres. Bonner Jahrb. 117 (1908), p. 1 ff.

E. E. = Ephemeris Epigraphica.

Eckhel = J. Eckhel, Doctrina Numorum Veterum. Vindobona, 1792.

Fayum = Fayum Towns and their Papyri, ed. by B. P. Grenfell, A. S. Hunt, and D. G. Hogarth. London, 1900.

Fleck, Jbb. = Neue Jahrbücher für Philosophie und Paedagogik.

Gö. Nachr. = Nachrichten von der Königlichen Gesellschaft der Wissenschaften zu Göttingen.

Grenf. Gk. Pap. = B. P. Grenfell, Greek Papyri. Oxford, 1896; also, B. P. Grenfell and A. S. Hunt, Greek Papyri, Series II. Oxford, 1897.

Head, Hist. Num. = B. V. Head, Historia Numorum. Ed. 2. Oxford, 1911.

Hopkins, Alex. Sev. = R. V. N. Hopkins, The Life of Alexander Severus. Cambridge, 1907.

Hunt. Coll. = Catalogue of Greek Coins in the Hunterian Collection, ed. by George Macdonald. Glasgow, 1899—.

I. G. = Inscriptiones Graecae.

I. G. R. = Inscriptiones Graecae ad Res Romanas pertinentes, Paris, 1901—.

J. H. S. = Journal of Hellenic Studies.

J. O. A. I. = Jahreshefte des Oesterreichen Archaeologischen Institutes in Wien.

K. W. Z. G. K. =Korrespondenzblatt der Westdeutschen Zeitschrift für Geschichte und Kunst.

Liebenam = W. Liebenam, Forschungen zur Verwaltungsgeschichte des Römischen Kaiserreichs. I Band, Die Legaten in den Römischen Provinzen von Augustus bis Diocletian. Leipzig, 1888.

Liebenam, Fasti = W. Liebenam, Fasti Consulares Imperii Romani. Bonn, 1909.

M. A. I. = Mitteilungen des Kaiserlichen Deutschen Archaeologischen Instituts, Athenische Abteilung.

M. N. D. P. V. = Mitteilungen und Nachrichten des Deutschen Palaestina-Vereins.

M. R. I. = Mitteilungen des Kaiserlichen Deutschen Archaeologischen Instituts, Römische Abteilung.

D. Magie, De Vocabulis Sollemnibus = David Magie, De Romanorum Iuris publici sacrique Vocabulis sollemnibus in Graecum Sermonem conversis. Teubner, 1905.

Marq. St. V. = J. Marquardt, Römische Staatsverwaltung. Ed. 2. Leipzig, 1881-1885.

Mél. Fac. Or. = Mélanges de la Faculté Orientale. Boyrouth.

Mitteis-Wilcken = L. Mitteis und U. Wilcken, Grundzüge und Chres-
tomathie der Papyrus-Kunde. Leipzig, 1912.

Mommsen, R. G. = Th. Mommsen, Römische Geschichte. Vol. 5, Die
Provinzen. Ed. 2. Berlin, 1885.

Mommsen, St. R. = Th. Mommsen, Römisches Staatsrecht. Ed. 3.
Berlin, 1887.

Muller, F. H. G. = Karl u. Theodor Müller, Fragmenta Historicorum
Graecorum. Vol. I, Paris, 1885.

N. C. = Numismatic Chronicle.

Notizie = Notizie degli Scavi.

Orelli = J. C. Orelli, Inscriptionum Latinarum Selectarum Amplissima
Collectio. Turici, 1828.

Ox. Pap. = The Oxyrynchus Papyri. Edited by B. P. Grenfell and
A. S. Hunt. London, 1898—.

P. A. E. S. = Publications of the Princeton University Archaeological
Expeditions to Syria in 1904-1905 and 1909. Leyden, 1907—.

P.-W. = Pauly-Wissowa, Real-Encyclopadie. Stuttgart, 1894—.

Pal. Explor. Fund = Palestine Exploration Fund.

Philol. = Philologus.

Prosop. = Prosopographia Imperii Romani. Berlin, 1897—.

R. B. = Revue Biblique Internationale.

R. E. A. = Revue des Études Anciennes.

R. G. K. = Römisch-germanisches Korrespondenzblatt.

R. N. = Revue Numismatique.

Rh. M. = Rheinisches Museum für Philologie. Neue Folge.

Schiller = H. Schiller, Geschichte der Römischen Kaiserzeit. Gotha,
1883.

Schürer, G. J. V. = E. Schürer, Geschichte des Jüdischen Volkes im
Zeitalter Jesu Christi. Ed. 3 and 4. Leipzig, 1902.

Sitz. Berl. Ak. = Sitzungsberichte der Kaiserlichen Preussischen
Akademie der Wissenschaften zu Berlin.

Stech, Senatores Romani = Bruno Stech, Senatores Romani qui
fuerint inde a Vespasiano usque ad Traiani exitum. Klio (1912),
Beiheft 10.

Stout, Govs. of Moesia = S. E. Stout, The Governors of Moesia.
Princeton, 1911.

Wadd. = Le Bas-Waddington, Voyage archéologique en Gréce et en
Asie Mineure, I-III. Paris, 1847-1877.

Wilcken, Gk. Ostr. = Ulrich Wilcken, Griechische Ostraka aus Aegyp-
ten und Nubien. Leipzig, 1899.

A. Wirth, Quaest. Sev. = A. Wirth, Quaestiones Severianae. Diss. 1888.

Z. D. P. V. = Zeitschrift des Deutschen Palaestina-Vereins.

Z. N. = Zeitschrift für Numismatik.

Zschr. Deutsch. Morg. Ges. = Zeitschrift der Deutschen Morgenländ. Gesellschaft.

- - - indicates the omission of part of an inscription.

? placed before a name, indicates that it is doubtful whether the person in question was governor or not.

? placed after a name, indicates that the name is not certain.

? used in connection with a date indicates that the time is uncertain.

[ ] inclosing a name, indicates that the person in question was not governor in my opinion.

The dates given for the consulships of the various governors are taken from Liebenam, Fasti.

TABLE OF CONTENTS

GOVERNORS OF SYRIA

Cn. Pompeius Collega[1] 69-70

Jos. B. J. VII, 3, 4 (§58-59); μόλις δ' αὐτῶν ἐδυνήθη τὰς ὁρμὰς ἐπισχεῖν Ναῖος Κολλήγας τις πρεσβευτής, ἀξιῶν ἐπιτρέψαι Καίσαρι δηλωθῆναι περὶ τῶν γεγονότων· τὸν γὰρ ἡγεμονεύοντα τῆς Συρίας Καισέννιον Παῖτον ἤδη μὲν Οὐεσπασιανὸς ἐξαπεστάλκει, συνέβαινε δὲ παρεῖναι μηδέπω.

This passage from Josephus shows that, in all probability, Collega, who was no doubt legate of a legion,[2] had been put in charge of Syria at the time of the departure of Mucianus in the autumn of 69.[3] The reference is to the autumn of 70,[4] before the arrival of the new consular legate Paetus.

L. Caesennius Paetus 70-72

(1) Jos. B. J. VII, 3, 4 (§58-59). See under Pompeius Collega.

(2) Mél. Fac. Or. II (1907), p. 337 = A. E. (1907), 193; Imp[erator] Ca[e]s. Vespa[sia]nus Aug. Pont. [Max] T[r]. P[ot]est. III P. [P.] Cos. IIII [cur. L. C]aesennio [Paeto] leg. Aug. pro[p]r. CCXXXIIII. (Near Beirût.)

(3) Jos. B. J. VII, 7, 1 (§219); ἤδη δὲ ἔτος τέταρτον Οὐεσπασιανοῦ διέποντος τὴν ἡγεμονίαν - - - - (§220) Καισέννιος Παῖτος, ὁ τῆς Συρίας ἡγεμὼν τότε καθεστηκώς - - - .

Consul in 61.

It is evident from the passage in Josephus (1) that Paetus was appointed governor of Syria by Vespasian, but had not yet arrived in the autumn of 70.[5] The inscription (2) from the mention of cos. IIII and trib. pot. III of Vespasian should be dated between Jan. 1, and July 1, 72.[6] The reference (3)

---

[1] Prosop. III, 65, 458.
[2] Similar cases of a legate of a legion acting as governor are found. See under A. Larcius Priscus, p. 19; and C. Julius Severus, p. 26.
[3] Liebenam p. 258. P.-W. III, 1308.
[4] Jos. B. J. VII, 3, 3. Schürer, G. J. V. I, p. 635.
[5] See under Pompeius Collega, n. 3.
[6] Cf. Stech, Senatores Romani p. 5, 19.

shows that Paetus was still governor in the fourth year of Vespasian, July 1, 72/73. During Paetus' term, Commagene was added to the province of Syria.[7]

Marius Celsus 73

B. C. H. XXVI (1902), p. 206 = A. E. (1903), 256; [Imp. Cae]sar Vespasianus Aug. [Pont.] Max. Trib. Potest. III[I·] [I]mp. X· [Cos. I]III· [Cos.] Designat. V· [P. P. Titus] Caesar Vespasianu[s I]mp. [I]II Trib. Potest. II· Co[s.] II Design. III . [C]ensores Designati su[b] |||| Mario Celso leg. Aug. pro pr. [p]e[r leg.]||||| et leg. |||||||||| opus cochli[dis d]e communi [imp(ensa)] fecerunt. (Near Aini on the Euphrates.)

The tr. pot. II of Titus dates the inscription July 1, 72/73 surely, while from the fact that Vespasian is cos. desig. V, and both are censores desig., the time would be the spring of 73, perhaps March.[8] Celsus no doubt succeeded Paetus, either at the end of 72, or the beginning of 73. Since he held office for a term of two or three years at least, he probably governed until Trajan took the province. Chapot, who edits the inscription, thinks that he was the consul of 62,[9] though possibly of 69.

M. Ulpius Traianus 76/77-79

(1) B. M. C. Galatia—(1899), p. 180, 239; Hunt. Coll. III (1905), p. 160, 139; T. Caesari. Imp. Pont. | ἐπὶ Τραιανοῦ 'Αντιοχέων ἐτ. ΕΚΡ.

(2) Stech (Senatores Romani p. 7, 34) gives part of a new inscription referred to by Dessau, Hermes XLV (1910), p. 9, n. 2; Trajan was legatus "[Imp. Titi C]aesa[ris D]ivi Vespas[ia]ni f. Vespa[siani Aug. pro pra]et. Syriae."

(3) Pliny, Paneg. 14, §1 ; Non incunabula haec tibi, Caesar,

[7] Marq. St. V. I, p. 399.
[8] Mommsen, St. R. II[3], p. 352. H. C. Newton, Cornell Stud. XVI (1901), p. 28ff. Acad. Inscr. et Belles-Lettres—Comptes Rendus (1912) Aug. Sept. p. 397.
[9] Stech, Senatores Romani p. 5, 20, believes that he was the consul of 62. It seems to me quite as probable that he was the consul of 69, a man who had had some experience in the East as leg. leg. XV Apoll. (Tacitus, A. XV, 25), and had been an active supporter of Otho in 69. (Prosop. II, 345, 223).

et rudimenta, cum puer admodum Parthica lauro gloriam patris
augeres - - -.

Consul suff. anno incert.

The date of the coins of Antioch (1), 125, according to the
Caesarian era, is autumn 76/77.[10] A new inscription (2)
shows that Trajan continued as governor through the middle
of 79, after the death of Vespasian in June.[11] In the same
year he was assigned to the proconsulship of Asia.[12] It seems
quite likely, from the notice in Pliny (3), that the "triumphalia
ornamenta," referred to by Stech (2) as in the inscription,
have to do with the Syrian governorship.

L. Ceionius Commodus   79/80

(1) B. M. C. Galatia—(1899), p. 272, 31; Hunt. Coll. III
(1905), p. 214, 25; R. N. II (1898), 2, p. 618, 7266; ἐπὶ
Κομόδου ΗΠΡ | Σελευκέων τῆς ἱερᾶς καὶ αὐτονομοῦ.
(2) A. J. Ph. VI (1885), p. 192; M. N. D. P. V. VII (1901),
p. 64, 29; I. G. R. III, 1356; E. Schwartz, Gö. Nachr. (1906),
p. 363; [ἔ]τους ΗΛΡ ὑ[πὲ]ρ τῆς τῶν Σ[εβαστῶν σωτηρίας] . . . | . . . ραι
ἀν[ε]στη[σ]αν πύλη[ν . . ἐκ τῶν ἰδ]ίων ἀν[εθ]ηκαν κα . . . . [Κ]ειων[ί]ου
Κομ[όδ]ου πρε[σβ. λεγ.[13]

Consul in 78.

From the coin with the date 188, it has been calculated,
reckoning according to the Actian era, which began Sep. 2,
31 B.C.,[14] that this Commodus should be dated 157/158 as
governor of Syria. The principal reason for choosing this era
seems to have been the fact that a C. Julius Commodus Orfi-
tianus is known in the middle of the second century, a legate
of Thrace and curator op. pub.[15] Dieudonné[16] has given
reasons, based on numismatic data, to show that the coin should
not be dated by the Actian era, but by the era of autonomy
of Seleucia. Kubitschek[17] also doubts the use of the Actian
era. It is especially noteworthy, that, aside from Commodus,

[10] P.-W. I, 650.
[11] Liebenam, Fasti p. 105.
[12] I. G. R. IV, 845.
[13] The name is filled out by Schwartz.
[14] O. Kaestner, De Aeris, p. 7, p. 22. Pick, Z. N. XIV (1887) p. 309ff.
[15] J. Klein, Rh. M. XXXV (1880), p. 317ff. Liebenam p. 382. Brünnow, Arabia III, p. 288, p. 300. Prosop. II, 187, 185.
[16] R. N. XIII (1909), p. 182ff.
[17] P.-W. I, 649.

no governor is mentioned on coins after Trajan in 76/77. There is besides epigraphical evidence for excluding Commodus from the date 157/158. C. I. L. III, D. CX gives Attidius Cornelianus as governor of Syria. The inscription is dated in the twentieth trib. pot. of Antoninus Pius (Dec. 10, 156/157), and "a. d. IV (month lost) - - ONO CAELIOSE," evidently denoting the cos. suffecti. The date may then fall within 156, after Dec. 10, in that case either Dec. 10, or 29, or in 157, probably after April since the consuls are suffecti. The latest date possible in 157 is Dec. 2. Therefore the dating of Commodus in 158 is impossible, since from 157 Cornelianus was governor for several years.[18] It is barely possible of course that the date of the coin could fall within the period Sep. 2, 157[19] to Dec. 2. Ritterling[20] also rejects C. Julius Commodus as governor of Syria in 157. The position of curator op. pub., held by Commodus in 161, could not, he says, follow the governorship of Syria at this time.[21] There is also an inscription from Palestine,[22] dated 161/169, which is assigned to this same Julius Commodus as governor of that province. But it is quite impossible that an official should go from a province of higher order to one of a lower.[23] The very reason then for dating our Commodus in 157/158, namely his presumable identity with C. Julius Commodus, is seen to have no weight.

Dieudonné,[24] after giving up the Actian area, chose to date the coin according to the era of autonomy very frequently used at Seleucia. He noted that L. Ceionius Commodus was consul in 78, so that he might well have held the governorship of Syria at this time. The date is 79/80.[25] Although an appointment to Syria so soon after the consulship is not usual, it is not unparalleled. The case of L. Vitellius is analogous.[26]

[18] See below, under the name, p. 30.
[19] See above, and n. 14.
[20] A. E. M. XX (1897), p. 28, note 68.
[21] R. no doubt means any consular province. The evidence of the inscriptions given in P.-W. IV, 1789, and A. E. (1904), 183, supports his view. There is one exception, C. I. L. XI, 3365.
[22] C. I. L. III, 6645.
[23] Domaszewski, Rangord., p. 180ff.
[24] Loc cit.
[25] Dieudonné, putting the year of the era in 110/109 B.C., dates the coin 78/79. The first year of the era however seems to be 109/108. See Dittenberger, Or. Gr. Inscr. I, p. 420, and Pick, Z. N. XIV, p. 310.
[26] Suet., Vitellius 2, §4. Schürer, G. J. V. I, p. 333.

An inscription[27] of Gerasa (2), dated 75/76 A.D., and containing the name of a Ceionius Commodus legatus—of a legion, as Schwartz thinks—may be referred with a fair degree of probability to this same man.[28]

T. Atilius Rufus   After 80-84

(1) C. I. L. III, D. XI; (Copiae) quae sunt in Pannonia sub T. Atilio Rufo - - - - Idibus Iunis L. Lamia Plautio Aeliano, C. Mario Marcello Octavio Publio Cluvio Rufo cos.

(2) Tacitus, Agr. 40; - - Syriam provinciam Agricolae destinari, vacuam tum morte Atilii Rufi consularis et maioribus reservatam.

Consul suff. anno incert.

The military diploma (1) shows that Rufus was governor in Pannonia June 13, 80, while the reference in Tacitus (2) to his death while governor of Syria is assigned to the year 84.[29]

M. Cornelius M. f. Gal. Nigrinus Curiatius Maternus

C. I. L. II, 6013; M. Cornelio M. f. G[al.] Nigrino Curiatio Materno cos. leg. Aug. pro pr. provinc. Moes. provinc. Syriae.

No. 3783 is very similar.

Consul suff. anno incert.

If these inscriptions are strictly correct, Maternus as governor of undivided Moesia must be dated before 90.[30] His term in Syria would then probably fall between the terms of Rufus and Iavolenus Priscus. An earlier date, though possible, is not likely, for the Syrian list is almost complete to this time.

C. Octavius Tidius Tossianus L. Iavolenus Priscus

Autumn 90/98

(1) C. I. L. III, 9960; C. Octavio Tidio Tossiano L. Iaoleno Prisco leg. leg. IV. Flav. leg. leg. III. Aug. iuridic. provinc. Brittanniae leg. consulari provinc. Germ. Superioris

[27] Schwartz (2) dates it according to the Pompeian era, and refers it to the Commodus consul in 78.

[28] Stech, Senatores Romani, p. 11, 70—the book came to my hand after this was written—notes most of the material which I have collected here; but comes to no conclusion.

[29] Prosop. I, 175, 1084. P.-W. II, 2094.

[30] Stout, Govs. of Moesia p. 20.

legato consulari provinc. Syriae proconsuli provinc. Africae pontifici P. Mutilius P. f. Cla. Crispins T. P. I. Amico Carissimo.

(2) C. I. L. XIII, 6821 = III, D. XXI; (Copiae) quae sunt in Germania Superiore sub L. Iavoleno Prisco. (Oct. 26, 90 A.D.)

(3) Pliny, Ep. VI, 15; - - - Is cum recitaret, ita coepit dicere, 'Prisce, iubes.' Ad hoc Iavolenus Priscus (aderat enim, ut Paulo amicissimus) 'ego vero non iubeo.' Cogita qui risus hominum, qui ioci. Est omnino Priscus dubiae sanitatis, interest tamen officiis, adhibetur consiliis atque etiam ius civile publice respondet - - -.

(4) Dig. XL, 2, 5; (Julianus) - - - ego, qui meminissem Iavolenum praeceptorem meum et in Africa et in Syria servos suos manumississe - - -.

Consul suff. ann. incert., between 83 and 90,[31] dates of his governorship of Numidia and Germania Sup., respectively; possibly in 87 as Pallu de Lessert[32] suggests, on the evidence of a fragment of Acta Fr. Arv.[33] which mentions a Priscus as consul.

A comparison of the inscriptions (1) and (2) shows that he must have been governor of Syria sometime after Oct. 26, 90. Now we have Quadratus as governor during the first years of the second century, and, as his successor, Palma. So in all probability Priscus would precede them. Furthermore the proconsulship was usually held about ten years after the consulship, in this period.[34] De Lessert[35] then makes him pro-consul of Africa by the year 97 or 98, preceding Marius Priscus. It is possible also to argue from the passage in Pliny (3) that Iavolenus Priscus,[36] who was then in Rome in 106 or 107, had become old and childish, and that his career of active service must have preceded that date.[37]

[31] Liebenam, Fasti p. 75.
[32] Fastes Prov. Afr. I, p. 167.
[33] Henzen, Acta Fr. Arv. CXX.
[34] Wadd. III, p. 659.
[35] Op. cit. p. 169.
[36] Op. cit. p. 167 and note 4.
[37] Stech, Senatores Romani p. 30, 193, fails to mention the governorship of Syria.

C. Antius Aulus Iulius A. F. Voltinia Quadratus
98/102-103 or 104

(1) Fränkel, Inschr. von Perg. II, 436; Γάιον ᾽Α[ντιον Αὐλ]ον Ἰούλιο[ν] Αὔλου υἱὸν [Κουαδρᾶτ]ον ὕπατο[ν] σεπτεμ[ουίρουμ ἐπουλώνουμ φρᾶτρε[μ ἀρουᾶλεμ] ----------- [πρεσβευτὴν καὶ ἀντι]στρά[τηγον Αὐτοκράτορος Νέρο]υα [Τραιανοῦ Καίσαρος Σεβαστοῦ Γερμανικοῦ Δακικοῦ Συρίας].

(2) Fränkel, Inschr. von Perg. II, 437 = I. G. R. IV, 374; [Α]ὖλον Ἰούλιον [Κουαδρᾶτον] ὕπατον, πρ[εσβευ]τ[ὴ]ν καὶ ἀντιστράτηγον Αὐτοκράτορος Νέρουα Τραιανοῦ Καίσαρος Σεβαστο[ῦ] Γερμανικοῦ Δακικοῦ Συρία[ς] Φοινείκης Κομμαγήνης - - -.

(3) Dittenberger, Or. Graec. Inscr. II, 486 = Fränkel II, 440; Γάιον ᾽Αντιον Αὖλον Ἰούλιον Αὔλου υἱὸν Κουαδρᾶτον, δὶς ὕπατον - - - - - πρεσβευτὴν καὶ ἀντιστράτηγον Αὐτοκράτορος Νέρουα Καίσαρος Τραιανοῦ Σεβαστοῦ Γερμανικοῦ ἐπαρχείας Συρίας - - -.

(4) M. A. I. XXIX (1904), p. 175, No. 19 = A. E. (1904), 193; ἡ βουλὴ καὶ ὁ δῆμος ἐτίμησε Γάιον ᾽Αντιον Αὖλον Ἰούλιον Αὔλου υἱὸν Οὐολτίνια Κουαδρᾶτον ὕπατον β' - - - πρεσβευτὴν καὶ ἀντιστράτηγον Αὐτοκράτορος Νέρουα Τραιανοῦ Καίσαρος Σεβαστοῦ Γερμανικοῦ ἐπαρχίας Συ[ρίας - - -.

Consul suff. in 93. Consul ord. in 105.

The inscription in Fränkel (1), which gives the first consulship only, puts the governorship of Syria before 105. Inscription (2), in the opinion of Fränkel, was put up during Quadratus' term in Syria. Since he is here legate of Trajan "Germanicus Dacicus," he can hardly have left the province before the beginning of 103.[38] But now Dittenberger[39] states: "Sed cum legatio Syriaca item anno 103 non antiquior sit - -." And so too v. Rohden[40] has "nicht vor 102." These inscriptions with "Germanicus Dacicus"[41] do show Quadratus as governor at the end of 102, but do not confine the beginning of his term to that date. It may have begun earlier, and in fact we have two inscriptions which go to show that it did. The one, published by Dittenberger himself (3), the other, by Schröder (4), show Quadratus as governor under Trajan "Germanicus" alone, without the "Dacicus." In view of this

[38] Fränkel, Inschr. von Perg. II, p. 299. Dittenberger (Or. Gr. Inscr. II, p. 117, n. 10.) prints Lyciacae and Lycia for Syriacae and Syria.
[39] Op. cit. n. 3, p. 116. Cf. n. 10.
[40] P.-W. I, 2565.
[41] With (2) cf. C. I. G. 3548.

omission it is possible to infer that Quadratus became governor as early as 98;[42] but surely before the fall of 102. The earliest possible date for the end of the governorship has been noted. It is quite reasonable to suppose, however, that Quadratus remained till late in 104, when he must have left to assume the consulship in 105. Early in that year we find him in Rome.[43]

A. Cornelius Palma 104-106/108

(1) I. G. R. III, 1291 ; ὑπὲρ σωτηρίας καὶ ὑγε(ί)ας Αὐτοκράτορος Νέρουα Τραιανοῦ Καίσαρος Σεβαστοῦ Γερμανικοῦ Δακικ[ο]ῦ, ἀγωγὸς ὑδάτων εἰσφερομένω[ν] εἰς Κάν[α]τα [ἐ]κ προνοίας [Κ]ορνηλίου Πάλμα πρέ[σ]β. Σεβ. ἀντιστρ. (El-Afineh) cf. No. 1273.

(2) Dio Cassius LXVIII, 14, 5 ; κατὰ δὲ τὸν αὐτὸν τοῦτον χρόνον καὶ Πάλμας τῆς Συρίας ἄρχων τὴν Ἀραβίαν τὴν πρὸς τῇ Πέτρᾳ ἐχειρώσατο καὶ Ῥωμαίων ὑπήκοον ἐποιήσατο.

Consul ord. in 99. Consul ord. II in 109.

Palma was no doubt the successor of Quadratus. The titles of Trajan in the inscriptions (1) indicate a date after 102. As Dio (2) tells us, Palma brought Arabia Petraea under Roman sway, in 105/106.[44] This date is borne out by the era of the capital, Bostra, which began March 22, 106.[45] How long after this he was governor is uncertain, quite likely up to the time of his second consulship.[46]

[Atticus]

Eusebius[47] tells us that Symeon, bishop at Jerusalem, was put to death ἐπὶ Τραιανοῦ Καίσαρας καὶ ὑπατικοῦ Ἀττικοῦ. The natural inference is, of course, that Atticus was governor of Judaea at this time. This is the opinion of Liebenam[48] and of Schürer.[49] Klebs,[50] however, and Groag[51] followed by

---

[42] Trajan took the title "Germanicus" in 97. See Liebenam, Fasti p. 107.
[43] Henzen, Acta Fr. Arv. CXLV, Jan. 3, 105.
[44] P.-W. IV, 1418 no. 279.
[45] Brünnow, Arabia, III, p. 303.
[46] So Stech, Senatores Romani, p. 71, 881.
[47] Hist. Eccl. III, 23, 3 and 6.
[48] Die Leg. p. 242.
[49] G. J. V. I, p. 645, 6. Schürer and Liebenam date him before Falco, governor from 107.
[50] Prosop. I, 353.
[51] P.-W. III, 2677.

Brünnow,[52] assert that, as there was no consular governor of Judaea at this time, Atticus must have been governor of Syria. This I do not believe. In the first place it was Symeon, bishop of Jerusalem, who was put to death. It is difficult to see what a governor of Syria would have to do with affairs at Jerusalem in the province of Judaea, quite distinct from Syria. Then too the only dates given for this event are 105 and 107.[53] But we have seen that Palma is pretty certainly established as governor of Syria in this time. Brünnow, who thinks that Palma was governor through 108, without any justification simply puts Atticus after him, though not with certainty.[54] Again consular legates in Palestine during the period before the great rebellion circa 133,[55] are not entirely unknown. Lusius Quietus[56] governor about 117, had been consul, and so perhaps had Falco,[57] governor before 110. Furthermore Judaea, after the rebellion was made a consular province.[58] Eusebius might very easily have made a mistake and called a praetorian governor, who came not so very long before the change, a consular. And Eusebius, writing, as he did, after 325, when the term "consular" had lost the restricted meaning which it had in earlier days,[59] could have used the word loosely to mean governor only. There seems then to be no compelling reason for assigning Atticus to Syria.

A. Larcius A. f. Quirina Priscus

(1) A. E., (1908), 237; I. O. M. A. Larcius A. f. Quir. Priscus, sevirum, decemvirum (sic) stilitib. iudicandis, quaestor provinciae Asiae, legatus Augusti. leg. IIII Scythicae, pro legato consulare provinc. Syriae, tribunus plebei, praetor, leg. provinciae Hispaniae Baeticae, praefectus frumenti dandi, legatus Augus. legionis II. Aug., legatus Aug. propr. exercitus Africae; V. S. L.

Cf. C. I. L. VIII, 17891.

[52] Arabia III, pp. 300 and 311.
[53] Schürer l. c. and references.
[54] Arabia III, pp. 287, 300 and 311.
[55] Schürer op. cit. I, p. 647ff.
[56] Op. cit. p. 647, 9.
[57] Op. cit. p. 645, 7.
[58] Domaszewski, Rangord, p. 179.
[59] P.-W. IV, 1139ff.

(2) C. I. L. VIII, 22382;

Via · [
Larcio · Prisc[o
Legato · August ·
Pro. Pr.

While legate of the Fourth Scythica, though not yet praetor, Priscus was "pro legato consulare provinc. Syriae" *i.e.* acting governor of Syria. (1). Mommsen's view,[60] that he belongs to Hadrian's time, based on the expression "leg. Aug. pr. pr. exercitus provinciae Afric.," is shown not conclusive by Pallu de Lessert,[61] who proves that the governorship of Numidia probably falls after 105, and before 172. Ritterling[62] would make Priscus legate of Syria at the time of the defeat of Attidius Cornelianus in 162. But if an argument may be properly based on the evidence of the style and form of an inscription, the broken milliarium of Priscus (2) should be dated early in the second century.[63] In general, an examination of the milliaria of C. I. L. VIII shows that the inscription of Priscus best agrees with those of Trajan's time or earlier, while after Hadrian, the legate's name does not appear in nearly so prominent a form.[64] Perhaps Priscus was acting governor when Palma subdued Arabia.[65]

Unknown 108/115?

C. I. L. III, 14387 d. -]b. m[—]r. prov[-] praet · 1[—] leg. III G[all] propr. pr[—] o. inter c[—] Nerva Traiano [—ab e]od. Imp. Parth[ico bello-] donis militarib. do[nato— Tr]aiani Aug. Germ. Da[cici prov—] item leg. propr. eius [provinciae] Syriae [posuit?] (Baalbek).

The inscription, in the ascending order, commemorates a man

[60] E. E. V, 696.
[61] Fastes Prov. Afr. I, p. 458ff.
[62] Rh. M. LIX (1904), p. 188ff. So too v. Premerstein in Klio XIII (1913), p. 79, n. 1. He would identify Priscus with the governor mentioned in C. I. L. III, 6715; but he overlooks the fact that by a better reading of the inscription in C. I. L. III, 14177, the governor is shown to be Geminius Marcianus of Arabia.
[63] Pallu de Lessert shows him to be after 105.
[64] C. I. L. VIII, 22190, 10186, 22348. A. E. (1907), 19. VIII, 10048, 22173, 10296, 10230. A. E. (1904), 21. VIII, 22629, 10238.
[65] Stech., Senatores Romani, p. 121, 1779, thinks him son of A. Larcius Lepidus, and senator under Trajan.

concerned in the Parthian war, at the earliest in 114,[66] if the restoration in the Corpus is correct, then legate apparently of some unknown province, then legate of Syria under Trajan. But there is hardly time for these offices after 114 and under Trajan. Besides Hadrian was the Syrian governor in 117, and quite likely earlier.[67] Trajan was "Optimus" in 114,[68] and though this title usually appears with his name, we do not find it here. Of course the governorship must follow that of Palma.[69]

Marinus

I. G. R. III, 1056, p. 397, l. 14/15; —secundum [vectigal]ia quae locavit antea Marinus praeses.[70] This is the translation of the Palmyrene part of the inscription which alone has the line on Marinus. In the original, the Greek word ἡγεμών, here rendered "praeses," is simply transliterated.

This title, as the editors observe,[71] probably denotes a governor or procurator. The word ἡγεμών, however, seems never to have been used as the title of an ordinary procurator. In Josephus there are cases of its use for the procurator of Judaea, who was however practically a governor, even commanding troops.[72] In the third century it is found as part of the title of a proc. vice praesidis.[73]

To denote a regular governor it is often used. In Egypt[74] it is used as the title of the praefectus. It is found in Galatia,[75] in Lycia and Pamphylia,[76] in Thrace.[77] As the title of a consular governor we find it in connection with πρεσβευτής[78] and with ἀντιστρατηγός.[79]

[66] Schiller I, p. 556.
[67] See below under Hadrian, p. 22.
[68] Liebenam, Fasti p. 107. And see below under Hadrian p. 22.
[69] See p. 18.
[70] Cf. Zschr. Deutsch. Morg. Ges. XLII (1884), p. 387, 15; Sitz. Berl. Ak. (1884), p. 430.
[71] I. G. R. III, p. 402.
[72] D. Magie, De Vocabulis Sollemnibus, p. 107, ref. to Jos. Ant. XVIII, 25 and 55.
[73] C. I. G. 2059; I. G. R. I, 10.
[74] I. G. R. I, 1057, 1098, 1154, 1175.
[75] I. G. R. III, 154.
[76] I. G. R. III, 342, 495, 668, 706.
[77] Liebenam p. 391 ff.
[78] I. G. R. III, 174.
[79] Wadd. 1842 a.

In literature we find the term frequently used for governors in general, from Josephus to Dio Cassius, who uses ἄρχων most frequently.[80] It seems reasonable then to conclude that Marinus was probably governor. It may be of significance also to note that in this inscription, where some regulation has been made, it was made in each case by an important person of consular rank, as Germanicus and Corbulo. Since the inscription is dated in 137, of course Marinus must have been governor previously. We know a Marinus who held high office early in the second century, L. Iulius Marinus consul in 101.[81] Before that he had been trib. mil. in the fourth Scythica in Syria, and governor of Lycia and Pamphylia.[82] Perhaps he was this Syrian governor. We may also think of his father, proconsul of Pontus and Bithynia,[83] and probably legate in Moesia Inferior in 97.[84]

P. Aelius P. f. Serg. Hadrianus 115-117

(1) Vita Hadriani 4, 1 ; - - - usus Plotinae quoque favore (Hadrianus) cuius studio etiam legatus expeditionis Parthicae tempore destinatus est.

(2) Dio Cassius LXIX, 1, 1 ; Ἀδριανὸς δε - - - - - τῇ τε Συρίᾳ ἐπὶ τῷ Παρθικῷ πολέμῳ προσετάχθη.

(3) Dio Cassius LXVIII, 33, 1 ; Τραιανὸς - - - - αὐτὸς μὲν ἐς τὴν Ἰταλίαν ὥρμησε πλεῖν, Πούπλιον δὲ Αἴλιον Ἀδριανὸν ἐν τῇ Συρίᾳ κατέλιπε μετὰ τοῦ στρατοῦ.

(4) Dio Cassius LXIX, 2, 1 ; ἦν δὲ, ὅτε ἀνηγορεύθη αὐτοκράτωρ, Ἀδριανὸς ἐν τῇ μητροπόλει Συρίας Ἀντιοχείᾳ, ἧς ἦρχεν.

(5) Vita Hadriani 4, 6 ; Quintum Iduum August. diem legatus Syriae (Hadrianus) litteras adoptionis accepit.

Consul suff. in 108.

That Hadrian was governor of Syria in 117, when Trajan left the East, is doubted by no one (3), (4),[85] (5). Many

[80] Jos., B. J. I, 20, 4; VII, 7, 1; Ant. XVI, 8, 6; XIX, 7, 2. Dio Chrys., Or. 46, cap. 14; Or. 43, cap. 11. Plutarch, Galba 6; 20; 22. Appian, B. C. V, 137; 144; Syr. 51. Lucian, De Morte Per. 14; Lucius 26. Aristides XLII, 533 (p. 789 Dindorf).
[81] Liebenam, Fasti p. 18.
[82] C. I. L. IX, 4965. A. E. (1899), 175.
[83] C. I. L. IX, 4965.
[84] A. E. (1913), 179.
[85] Cf. Zonaras XI, 22B, and 23.

however think that only at that time was he appointed governor, while before that he was a legatus and comes of Trajan in the war.[86] But Dio does not necessarily imply that Hadrian was made governor so late. In fact a fair interpretation of his words in (2) would seem to me to show that Hadrian began to govern at the opening of the Parthian campaigns. This is the view of Liebenam,[87] and v. Rohden[88] admits that it is possible. The statement in the Vita (1) may mean that Hadrian was appointed governor. The term "legatus" is often so used in these lives,[89] while "comes" in late times is very generally used to denote legates of the emperor when he took the field. Trajan undoubtedly needed an able man whom he could trust, to take charge of Syria, especially at Antioch, his base[90] for the campaign of invasion. Hadrian was surely a man for the place. His holding this office would well explain the fact that he does not appear in the actual fighting, though many other legates are named.[91] I am inclined then to date the beginning of his term at the time of the beginning of the war.[92 and 93]

[86] Schiller I, p. 603. G. W. Weber, Die Adopt. Kais. Hadr., p. 25. Dierauer, in Budinger Untersuch., p. 159. E. Groag, M. R. I. XIV (1899), p. 276.
[87] Die Leg. pp. 278, and 379.
[88] P.-W. I, 499.
[89] Pesc. Niger 6; L. Verus 9; Alex. Sev. 52.
[90] Schiller I, p. 556.
[91] Op. cit. p. 557ff.
[92] The old view was that the war began in 114 (Dierauer, in Büdinger Untersuch., p. 160. Schiller I, p. 556).
[93] Mommsen (R. G. V, 398 and note 1) puts the beginning in 115. He is followed by Dittenberger (Or. Gr. Inscr. II, p. 221, n. 17) and Niese (R. G.² p. 206).
Boissevain (ed. of Dio Cassius, Vol. III, p. 209 and notes) thinks Mommsen wrong—incorrectly, I believe—because Xiphilinus says that Trajan was granted the title "Optimus" after the Armenian campaign; a title granted by Sep. 1, 114. But Xiphilinus is incorrect in connecting the title with the campaign, for it seems clear that Trajan was given the title by the end of 113 (C. I. L. III, 15021 = J. O. A. I. XI (1908) Beiblatt p. 71, fig. 49). And in any case Trajan had the title before he left Rome for the East. Coins in Cohen (II, p. 21, no. 40; cf. no. 307) read; Imp. Traiano Optimo Aug. Ger. Dac. P. M. Tr. P./Augusti Profectio, plainly referring to Trajan's departure.

[Sex. Erucius Clarus]

Liebenam[94] inserts Clarus in his list as governor of Syria in 116, but without any reason except that he was a legate of Trajan in the Parthian war. Worse still Liebenam contradicts himself by making Hadrian's term,[95] 114-117, cover this same period.

L. Catilius Severus Iulianus Claudius Reginus 117-119

(1) R. E. A. XV (1913), p. 270:
L. Cat[i]lio. C[n. f. Cla]u. Sev[e]ro I[u]lia[no] Claudio Reg[i]no co[s II pr]o cos. provin[c.] Af[ri]cae . . . . . r. p . . et . . l. [l]eg. Aug. [pro praet.] pro[v. Syriae. l]eg. Aug. pr[o] pr. Arm[eniae m]aior[is e]t M[in]or[is] et Ca[p]padoci[ae p]raef. aer[a]r. m[ilitar.] leg. leg. XX[II] Primi[g. p. f. c]urato[ri . . . . le]g. pro pr. [p]rov[i]nc[iae] Asiae [VI vir. eq. R.] pr. u]rb. q]uaes[t. prov. As]iae d. d. [p. p.].

(2) C. I. L. X, 8291; and R. E. A. XV (1913), p. 272; L.]Catilio. Cn. f. [Clau.] [Sever]o Iuliano. C. R[egi]no, cos. II., [pr]ocos. provinc. Afr[ic]ae, leg. Aug. pr. p[r. provi]nciae Syriae, et provinciae Cappad[ociae] et Armeniae Maior. et Minor., VII vir. epu[lon., do]nis militaribus donato a Divo Tr[aiano] etc.

(3) Vita Hadriani 5, 10; Quibus (reliquiis Traiani) exceptis et navi Romam dimissis ipse Antiochiam regressus praepositoque Syriae Catilio Severo per Illyricum Romam venit.

(4) A. E. (1911), 95 = B. A. R. (1911), p. 137;
AT VIII K
L. Vips]tano Messalla
L. Cat]ilio. Severo
. . . . . no. Cos.

The identification of L. Catilius Severus with C. Atilius Iulianus Rufinus has recently been pretty well established by A. Merlin.[96] The proof is based largely on the governorship of Cappadocia and the Armenias, the similarity of names, and the proconsulate of Africa. It is remarkable also that, of the two consulships of Rufinus, neither has ever been satisfactorily

[94] Die Leg. p. 380.
[95] Op. cit. pp. 379, and 278.
[96] R. E. A. XV (1913), p. 268ff.

placed,[97] while the two of Severus are now definitely known. The second consulship of Catilius Severus, as has long been known, was in the year 120.[98] A recently discovered inscription (4) places him as consul suffectus to Pedo Vergilianus;[99] who perished in office during the earthquake at Antioch[100] in 115. This inscription, which has been overlooked by Merlin, also shows us that "Iulianus" was a part of the name of Catilius Severus, and thus adds proof for the identification of Rufinus and Severus. In the last line I would read, for ".... no," "[Iulia]no."[101]

Since Severus held the consulship in 115, his term as governor of the Armenias and Cappadocia can not have begun in 114 as Merlin suggests. If he were the sole governor of the short-lived province, as seems probable, his term would then have begun late in 115,[102] or in 116, after his consulship. This

[97] C. I. L. X, 8291 identifies him with L. Cuspius Rufinus cos. of 142, and suggests that he then held his second consulship.
[98] Liebenam, Fasti p. 20.
[99] Op. cit. p. 19.
[100] Dio Cassius LXVIII, 25, 1.
[101] The fact that Liebenam has placed the governorship of Rufinus in Cappadocia and the Armenias before that of M. Iunius, governor of Cappadocia, and has placed his term in Syria even before that of Hadrian (he is followed in this by Brünnow, Arabia III p. 300 and 311), might seem to make the identification of Rufinus and Severus impossible, since they are thus separated in time. But the evidence at hand, even before the publication of Merlin's inscription, proves Liebenam incorrect. M. Iunius was legate of Cappadocia at the very beginning of Trajan's eastern campaign (Dio Cassius LXVIII, 19). Rufinus, preceding Iunius, would then have held the governorship of Cappadocia and the Armenias before the actual formation of the provinces, which was accomplished probably in 115. (See below, and note 103.) This is of course impossible. Then Liebenam, further, while he recognizes that the Syrian governorship follows that of Cappadocia and the Armenias (Pallu de Lessert, Fastes Prov. Afr. I, 183, puts that of Syria before, for some unknown reason), is able to date the former before the governorship of Hadrian. But since, as we have seen, the Cappadocian-Armenian governorship can not have begun before 115, there can be little doubt that the Syrian governorship must follow that of Hadrian and Catilius Severus his successor. So, even on the basis of the old evidence alone, Severus and Rufinus are brought into juxtaposition in their governorship of Syria, and there is then no chronological barrier to their identification.
[102] Fr. Cumont, Bull. Ac. Roy. Belg.-Lettr. (1905), p. 208, made Rufinus governor 115-117.

25

would accord very nicely with the idea of Mommsen[103] that the Armenian campaign did not begin before 115. From the evidence of the Vita (3) we should naturally conclude that Severus was withdrawn from Armenia, which Hadrian gave up,[104] and was put over Syria in the fall of 117.[105] This evidence supported, as it is, by the inscriptions, leaves no room for the doubt, expressed by Stech,[106] that Severus was ever governor of Syria. Severus' term extended very likely through part of 119,[107] when he must have left to take up the consulship in 120.

C. Publicius Marcellus   Circa 132

C. I. G. 4034 = I. G. R. III, 175 ; Γ. I. Σεουῆρον - - - ἡγεμόνα λεγιῶνος τετάρτης Σκυθικῆς καὶ διοικήσαντα τὰ ἐν Συρίᾳ πράγματα, ἡνίκα Πουβλίκιος Μάρκελλος διὰ τὴν κείνησιν τ[ῆ]ν Ἰουδαικὴν μεταβεβήκει ἀπ[ὸ] Συρίας, ἀνθύπατον Ἀχαίας, πρὸς πέ[ν]τε ῥάβδους πεμφθέντα εἰς Βειθυνίαν διορθωτὴν καὶ λογιστὴν ὑπὸ θεοῦ Ἁδριανοῦ, etc.; cf. C. I. G. 4033 = Dittenberger., Or. Gr. Inscr. II, 543 = I. G. R. III, 174. Consul suff. in May, 120.

Marcellus was governor of Syria at the outbreak of the rebellion of the Jews, which took place, at least to any serious extent, in 132.[108] As leader of the Syrian legions, he went into Judaea to the assistance of the governor Rufus.[109] How long he remained, we do not know, but quite likely until the end of the rebellion.

C. Iulius Severus[110]   Circa 132

(See under Publicius Marcellus for inscriptions.)

Severus as legate of IV Scythica[111] was substitute governor during the absence of Marcellus. If Dio[112] is correct in assign-

---

[103] See under Hadrian note 93.
[104] Schiller I, p. 606.
[105] W. Weber, Unters. z. Gesch. d. K. Hadr. p. 58.
[106] Senatores Romani p. 43, 302.
[107] Liebenam p. 380.
[108] Schürer, G. J. V. I, p. 682. Schulz, Leben des K. Hadrian p. 82 and note 235, thinks its actual beginning was in 130.
[109] Schürer op. cit. p. 689. Eusebius, Hist. Eccl. IV, 6, 1.
[110] On the name see Dittenberger, Or. Gr. Inscr. II, 543 and note 1.
[111] It is noteworthy that the only other "pro legato consulari" of whom we have any detailed information, Larcius Priscus, was also legate of the IV Scythica. See Ritterling in Rh. M. LIX (1904) p. 188ff.
[112] LXIX, 14, 4.

ing Severus' mission in Bithynia to about the end of the Jewish war, he must have left Syria during that war, and perhaps early, since he was appointed proconsul of Achaia between his Syrian and Bithynian positions. Possibly in this fact there might be a slight indication that Publicius Marcellus had returned to Syria before the end of the war.

Sex. Minicius Faustinus C.? Iulius C.? f. Serg. Severus
135 or 136/138

C. I. L. III, 2830, and supp. 9891 ; [Se]x. M[i]nicio Faustino [C.?] I[uli]o [C.? f]il. Serg. Severo [v. c.] - - - - - praetor., leg. leg. XIIII. Gemin[ae, l]eg. pr. pr. Imp. Traiani Hadria[n]i Aug. p[r]ovinciae Dacia[e], cos., leg. pr. p[r.] provinciae Moesia[e] Inferioris, leg. pr. pr. provinciae Brittaniae, leg. pr. pr. [pr]ovinciae Iudeae [le]g. pr. pr. [provi]nciae Suriae, huic [senatus a]uctore [Imp.] Caes. [Tra]iano Hadrian[o Au]g. ornamenta triu[mp]halia decrevit ob res in [Iu]dea prospere ge[st]as. [d.] d.
Consul suff. in Oct. 127.

From the fact that the inscription was set up while Hadrian was still alive it is evident that the governorship of Syria must come before the middle of 138.[113] From the form of the last part, where the mention of the "ornamenta" follows the legateship of Syria, it is a fair conclusion that the term in Syria came very soon after that in Judaea. The rebellion, which Severus put down in Judaea, lasted well into 134, and perhaps into 135.[114] So then Severus probably became governor of Syria in 135 or 136, if we allow some little time after the end of the rebellion for settling affairs in Judaea.

L. Burbuleius L. f. Quir. Optatus Ligarianus
Circa 145

C. I. L. X, 6006; L. Burbuleio L. f. Quir. Optato Ligariano, cos., sodal. Aug., leg. Imperat. Antonini Aug. Pii pro pr. prov. Syriae, in quo honor[e] decessit, leg. eiusdem et Divi Hadriani pro pr. prov. Cappad., cur. oper. locor. q. publ., praef. aerar. Saturn., pro cos. Sicil., logiste Syriae, legat. leg. XVI. Fl. Firm. etc.

---

[113] Liebenam, Fasti p. 107.
[114] Schürer, G. J. V. I, p. 695 ff. W. Weber, Unters. z. Gesch. d. K. Hadr. p. 276.

Consul suff. anno incert. before 138.
He was governor of Cappadocia at the earliest in the last part of 137, since Fl. Arrianus was still góvernor in that year.[115] It seems reasonable to suppose that he went from this position directly to that of legate of Syria. If there is truth in the statement of the Vita[116] that the emperor kept good governors in their positions "septenis et novenis annis," perhaps we should put the beginning of his Syrian term circa 145.

Unknown   Circa 135/150

Lucian, De Morte Peregr. cap. 14; πλὴν ἀλλ᾽ ὁ Περεγρῖνος ἀφείθη ὑπὸ τοῦ τότε τῆς Συρίας ἄρχοντος, ἀνδρὸς φιλοσοφίᾳ χαίροντος, ὃς συνεὶς τὴν ἀπόνοιαν αὐτοῦ καὶ ὅτι δέξαιτ᾽ ἂν ἀποθανεῖν, ὡς δόξαν ἐπὶ τούτῳ ἀπολίποι, ἀφῆκεν αὐτὸν οὐδὲ τῆς κολάσεως ὑπολαβὼν ἄξιον.

This govêrnor of Syria, whose name is not given, may perhaps be dated very roughly. Peregrinus cremated himself at the Olympian games in 165 or 167.[117] It was eight or twelve years before this that he criticised Herodes Atticus for supplying water to Olympia,[118] i.e. 159 (157) or 155 (153).[119] Now between this affair and his adventures in Syria,[120] surely ten years must have elapsed. A "terminus ante quem" for the governor then would be 150. But since this affair was among his early adventures[121], and he was an old man when he died,[122] the event might fall ten or fifteen years earlier. The governor is probably to be dated between 135 and 150.

Sulpicius Iulianus   149?

(1) B. C. H. XXVI (1902), p. 165 = A. E. (1903), 252; Imp. T. Aelio [Ha]d[ri]ano Antonino Aug. Pio P. P. vexil.

---

[115] I. G. R. III, 111. Prosop. I, 243.
[116] Vita Ant. Pii 5.
[117] Lucian, De Morte Peregr. 36. Eusebius, "Chron. aus dem Armen." in "Gk. Schr. der erst. 3 Jahrh." p. 222. Nissen, Rh. M. XLIII (1888), p. 254.
[118] Lucian, op cit. 19 and 20.
[119] Schulthess, Herodes Atticus pp. 18 and 19. Frazer (Paus. vol. IV, p. 74) puts the completion of the water works in 150 or 151.
[120] Lucian, op. cit. 14-19.
[121] Op. cit. 9-14.
[122] Op. cit. 8; 33; 37.

leg. IIII Scy[th. et leg.] XVI F. F., su[b] Sul[picio?] Iuliano ||||||||. (Seleucia Pieria.)

(2) Wadd. 2306 = I. G. R. III, 1274; --- [Αὐτοκρ]άτορος Καίσαρος [Τ. Αἰλίου Ἀδριαν]οῦ Ἀντωνείνου Σε[βαστοῦ, τοῦ ἡμῶν κ]υρίου, καὶ Αὐρηλίου [Οὐήρου Καίσαρος, υ]ἱοῦ αὐτοῦ καὶ λοι[πῶν αὐτοῦ τέκνω]ν καὶ σύνπαντος [οἴκου Σεβαστοῦ καὶ τῆ]ς ἱερωτάτης συνκλή[του Ῥώμης καὶ τῆς ἡγ]εμονίας Ῥωμαίων [. . . . . . ἐπὶ] Ἀπικίου Ἰουλιανοῦ [ὑπατικοῦ - -

Both these inscriptions refer to governors of Syria, during the reign of Antoninus Pius, who should, I have no doubt, be identified. We have in (1), Sul[picio?] Iuliano; in (2) l. 9, ... ἐπὶ] ΑΠΙΚΙΟΥΙΟΥΛΙΑΝΟΥ. Surely the A in this poorly preserved inscription should be read Λ, and the line filled out, - - - - ἐπὶ Σου]λπικίου Ἰουλιανοῦ. If Waddington's idea, that his inscriptions 2307 and 2306 belong together, is correct, our governor is to be dated in 149.

?M. Cassius Apollinaris?

Mél. Fac. Or. IV (1909), p. 543 = A. E. (1909), 115; ΜΚ·ΑΣΑΠΟΛΥΠ = M. Κασ(σίου) Ἀπολ(λειναρίου) ὑπ(ατεύοντος or -ατικοῦ).

This inscription, found in such a position that it could not have been visible, in the opinion of the editors was cut by soldiers engaged in construction work. They would naturally carve the name of their commander, the governor of Syria. An Apollinaris was consul suffectus in 150;[123] but it does not seem at all probable that, as such, he would be mentioned in an inscription of this character from Syria. It is, however,. possible that he is here referred to as governor of Syria.

D. Velius Fidus

C. I. L. III, 14387 e; D. Velio Fido leg. Aug. pr. . . . . . (Baalbek).

It seems probable that Fidus is here mentioned as a governor of Syria. It is reasonable, with the editor of the Corpus, to identify him with Velius Fidus, a pontifex in Rome in 155,[124] for most of the inscriptions found with this one are of the first and second centuries.

[123] Liebenam, Fasti p. 22.
[124] C. I. L. VI, 2120.

[C. Iulius Severus]

Severus was not a governor of Syria and Palestina, as Liebenam[125] would have it, but of Syria Palestina.[126]

[C. Iulius Commodus Orfitianus]

On this governor see above, p. 13, under L. Ceionius Commodus, year 79/80.

L. Attidius Cornelianus   156/157-162

(1) C. I. L. III, D. CX; [Imp. Cae]s., Divi Hadria[ni f., Divi Traiàni Parthici] n., Divi Nervae [pron., T. Aei]ius Hadrianus An[toninus Aug. Pius] P. M., Tr. Pot. XX., Imp. I[I, cos III, P. P.] - - - - (troops) sunt in Suria sub Attidio Corneliano leg. - - - a. d. IV . . . . no C. Aelio Se . . . . [cos.].

(2) C. I. L. III, 6658; Imp. Caesari Divi Antonini fil., Divi Hadriani nep., Divi Traiani Parth. pronep., Divi Nervae abnep., L. Aurelio Vero Au[g.], Pontif. Max., Trib. Pt. I[I], cos. II., P. P., coh. I. Fl. Cha[l.] eq. sag. sub Attidio Corneliano leg. Au[g.] pr. pr. per Aelium Herculanum prae[f.] (Near Damascus).

(3) Vita Ant. Philos. 8, 6; Fuit eo tempore etiam Parthicum bellum quod Vologessus, paratum sub Pio, Marci et Veri tempore indixit, fugato Attidio Corneliano qui Syriam tunc administrabat.

Consul anno incert. 150/157.

Cornelianus was governor of Arabia in 150.[127] The military diploma, dated in the twentieth tribunician power of Antoninus. Pius 156/157 (1), shows that he was governor of Syria by Dec. 2, 157 at the latest. Even after his defeat by the Parthians which was in 161,[128] or perhaps early in 162,[129] he was retained as governor,[130] probably until the arrival of

[125] Die Leg. p. 382, 40.
[126] Schürer, G. J. V. I, p. 643, note 1.
[127] Brünnow, Arabia III, p. 287.
[128] Schiller I, p. 639.
[129] C. H. Dodd, N. C. (1911), p. 216. E. Ritterling, Rh. M. LIX (1904), p. 190, n. 2.
[130] Ritterling (op. cit. p. 190) assumes that Cornelianus was at once recalled, apparently for the purpose of inserting A. Larcius Priscus as governor at this point. (On Priscus see above, p. 19.)

Verus in the East. This is shown by the inscription (2), dated in 162, and set up in honor of Verus alone, a thing which would hardly have been done unless word had already come that Verus was personally to oppose the Parthians. This plan was doubtless only made after the serious defeat of the Syrian legions.[131] It may perhaps be that it is this Cornelianus who was enrolled in a priestly college in 190 A.D., and who died in 198.[132]

M. Annius M. f. Libo   Circa 162/163

Vita Veri 9, 2; Verum illud praecipuum quod cum Libonem quendam patruelem suum Marcus legatum in Syriam misisset, atque ille se insolentius quam verecundus senator efferet, dicens ad fratrem suum se scripturum esse, si quid forte dubitaret, nec Verus praesens pati posset, subitoque morbo notis prope veneni exsistentibus interisset, visum est nonnullis, non tamen Marco, quod eius fraude putaretur occisus.

Libo was sent out probably as legate of Syria, and not to serve as legate or comes of Verus, with whom he was apparently not on good terms. This is the opinion of Liebenam,[133] while E. Ritterling[134] doubts if he was governor. Libo may well have been the immediate successor of Cornelianus in 162 or early 163.

Cn. Iulius Cn. fil. Verus   164/165

(1) C. I. L. III, 199; Imp. Caes. M. Aurel. Antoninus Aug. Armeniacus, et Imp. Caes. L. Aurel. Verus Aug. Armeniacus, viam fluminis vi abruptam, interciso monte, restituerunt per Iul. Verum leg. pr. pr. provinc. Syr. et amicum suum. Impendis Abilenorum.

(2) C. I. L. III, 8714; Cn Iulio. Cn. fil. Vero. cos. desig. II, augur (C. I. L. III, 2732) leg. A[ug.] pr. pr. provinc. Syriae, leg. Aug. pr. pr. provinc. Brittaniae, leg. Aug. pr. pr. provinciae German. Inferioris, praef. aerari Saturni, leg. leg. XXX Ulpiae, praetor., tribu[no] plebis, etc.

Consul suff. circa 150/155. Consul suff. II, after 164.

That the two inscriptions (2) belonged together was first

---

[131] Stein, P.-W. III, 1841ff.
[132] C. I. L. VI, 2004. Liebenam p. 383.
[133] Die Leg. p. 383.
[134] K. W. Z. G. K. XXII (1903), 214ff.

seen by Ritterling;[135] and at about the same time, by Haverfield.[136] The identification has supplied a great deal of information about Verus. From this and some other inscriptions of Britain,[137] Ritterling calculated that Verus was governor of Germania Inferior circa 153-157, and of Britain circa 157-160.[138] According to the imperial titles[139] of our inscription (1), Verus held the governorship of Syria between the end of 163 and the summer of 165. If the title "Armeniacus" of Marcus Aurelius be rightfully assigned, the inscription is most reasonably to be dated at the earliest in the middle of 164.[140]

Gaius Iulius[141] Avidius Cassius   165-175

(1) Wadd. 2525 = I. G. R. III, 1113 ; ὑπὲρ σωτηρίας καὶ νίκης τῶν κυρίων Αὐτοκρατόρων Μ. Αὐρηλίου ᾿Αντονείνου καὶ Λ. Αὐρηλίου Οὐήρου Σεβ., Φαινήσιοι ἀφιέρωσαν ἐπὶ ᾿Αουιδίου Κασσίου πρεσβ. Σεβ. ἀντ., ἐφεστῶτος ᾿Εγνατίου Φούσκου ἑκατοντάρχου λεγ. γ´ Γαλλικῆς. (Phaena).

(2) Wadd. 2112 = I. G. R. III, 1261 ; ὑπὲρ σωτηρίας τοῦ κυρίου Αὐτοκράτορος Καίσαρος Μ. Αὐρηλίου ᾿Αντωνείνου Σεβαστοῦ καὶ τοῦ σύνπαντος οἴκου καὶ νείκης, ἔτους ἐνδεκάτου, ἐπὶ ᾿Αουιδίου Κασσίου τοῦ λαμπροτάτου ὑπατικοῦ - - - . (Nela).

[135] K. W. Z. G. K. XXII (1903), p. 214ff.
[136] Proc. Soc. Ant. Scot. XXXVIII (1904), p. 454ff.
[137] A. E. (1903), 360; (1904), 229.
[138] Haverfield (op cit.) gives a new inscription of the year 158, during Verus' term in Britain. Very probably he is also commemorated in C. I. L. VII, 967.
[139] Liebenam, Fasti p. 108.
[140] P.-W. III, 1840, 1846 and 2294. C. H. Dodd in N. C. (1911), pp. 217, 223, and 235.
[141] The name in the inscriptions and in literature appears simply as "Avidius Cassius." Wilcken, Gk. Ostr. II, 939, gives the praenomen "Gaius." That this is correct is rendered probable by the fact that Cassius' father's praenomen was also "Gaius." (C. I. L. III, 6025; Dio Cassius LXXI, 22; Prosop. I, 186, 1165.) A papyrus (5) gives the name "Iulius" without "Gaius." It refers to Cassius as emperor, during his revolt. If the name is correctly given, it may have been part of his name originally, or perhaps it was added at the time of his revolt. Cassius seems to have hoped for support on the ground that he was more fitted than Marcus to rule during those warlike times (Schiller I, p. 658), and what more natural than that he should have assumed as his name that of the great Dictator?

32

Other inscriptions dating between (1) and (2); I. G. R. III, 1114; 1179; 1270; 1226; 1261. A. A. E. S. III, no. 381; P. A. E. S. III, A, 2, p. 91, no. 155.

(3) Dio Cassius LXXI, 2, 2; ὁ οὖν Λούκιος ἐλθὼν ἐς Ἀντιόχειαν καὶ πλείστους στρατιώτας συλλέξας, καὶ τοὺς ἀρίστους τῶν ἡγεμόνων ὑφ᾽ ἑαυτὸν ἔχων, αὐτὸς μὲν ἐν τῇ πόλει ἐκάθητο διατάττων ἕκαστα καὶ τὰς τοῦ πολέμου χορηγίας ἀθροίζων, Κασσίῳ δὲ τὰ στρατεύματα ἐπέτρεψεν.

(4) P. A. E. S. III, A, 5, 666; F(ines) M(arci) Herp(i): iusso (A)vidi C(a)ssi co(n)s(ularis) per F(a)(v)onium Priorem pr(a)efectum.

(5) Bull. Inst. Egypt VII[a](1896), p. 123; L a Αὐτοκράτορος Καίσαρος Ἰουλίου Ἀουιδίου Κασίου παχὼν ὀγδώῃ.

Consul suff. in May 161/168 surely; probably 161/164.[142]

The inscriptions record Avidius Cassius as governor of Syria from early 169 (1), at the latest, to 171/172 (2). It seems probable however that he was governor earlier, while commander in the Parthian war.

Now this Eastern war had two quite distinct phases. In 163 Armenia was conquered under the leadership of Statius Priscus, governor of Cappadocia.[143] In 164 while Armenian affairs were doubtless being organized, there was little fighting. This was the bellum Armeniacum.[144] Then in 165 Verus and Marcus became Imp. III, and Verus took the title Parthicus Maximus.[145] In this year falls the serious fighting with the Parthians. To this no doubt Dio Cassius refers (3), as Dodd well says.[146] Mommsen very reasonably makes Cassius governor of Syria while in command of the war.[147] It seems very probable also that, since the first stage was under a governor's direction, the second stage should be managed similarly. In both cases then, the regular and natural commander of the region would be chief commander in the war, under Verus.

Ritterling[148] has attempted to show that Cassius was governor of Arabia during the war. To this end he has assumed that Cassius was consul only shortly before 166, although, as

[142] C. I. L. III, D. 47. Prosop. I, 186, 1165.
[143] C. I. L. VI, 1523.
[144] Schiller I, p. 640 and n. 3. P.-W. I, 2293/4. Dodd, N. C. (1911), pp. 234 and 256.
[145] Liebenam, Fasti p. 108.
[146] N. C. (1911), p. 254.
[147] R. G. V, 406.
[148] Rh. M. LIX (1904), p. 194.

33

a matter of fact, he may as well have been consul in 161. He then proceeds to support his view by an appeal to a passage in Lucian,[149] where Cassius is mentioned in connection with a third legion, which Ritterling believes to be the Third Cyrenaica. At the same time he has omitted to mention the passage in Dio Cassius (3), which shows that Cassius was chief commander in the war. It is absurd to think of Cassius, evidently the chief general under Verus, as legate of Arabia in this period. Moreover if it be true, as has been suggested by Stout,[150] that Cassius was governor of Moesia Superior in the early sixties, he can not have been governor of Arabia.

v. Premerstein,[151] in tracing the career of Cassius, following Ritterling in part, has concluded likewise that Cassius, consul only shortly before 166, can not have been governor of Syria during the war. He believes that Cassius was at that time leg. legionis, probably of the Third Gallica.[152] The Vita shows,[153] he thinks, that Cassius may well have been a dux exercitus around 168 in Lower Pannonia; but only at the end of 168 or at the beginning of 169 can he have reached the position of governor of Syria. It seems to me that the statements of v. Premerstein are based on scant evidence. He assumes, as does Ritterling, that Cassius was consul only shortly before 166, and fails to take into account the very important passage in Dio Cassius (3).

Domaszewski,[154] from the evidence of a newly discovered inscription (4), supposes Cassius to have been governor of Arabia, under Antoninus Pius. There is little basis for this view. The provenience of the inscription is by no means surely Arabian territory. It was found at il-Kefr,[155] some 18 km. to the north of Bostra in territory forming the borderland between Arabia and Syria,[156] but territory which at the time probably belonged to Syria, for an inscription of Martius Verus, the successor of Cassius in the governorship of Syria,

---

[149] Quomodo Historia—, 31.
[150] Govs. of Moesia p. 27.
[151] Klio XIII (1913), p. 78ff.
[152] Cf. note 149.
[153] Cf. note 150.
[154] R. G. K. (1909), p. 36.
[155] P. A. E. S. III, A, 5, 666.
[156] Brünnow, Arabia III, p. 266.

has been found there.[157] Moreover the title consularis, while by exception it is applied to praetorian governors, properly belongs to the governor of a consular province. Then too it may be here an evidence of the maius imperium of Cassius.[158] It seems rather strange however that the maius imperium of the Syrian governor should override the powers of the regular Arabian governor in so simple a matter as the fixing of a boundary stone, and I am inclined to think that it was placed under the direction of Cassius governor of Syria.

That Cassius held a maius imperium over the "Oriens," during the time of his governorship in Syria, has long been recognized.[159] At what time he received it, however, is not known; but surely at the earliest on the withdrawal of Verus from the East in the middle of 166.[160] The earliest date, at which we can be reasonably sure that he held it, is 169. This is shown by an inscription of that year found at Salkhad in territory regularly assigned to Arabia.[161] In Zonaras[162] and in the epitome of Dio by Xiphilinus,[163] the statement that Cassius received maius imperium follows after the account of the death of Verus, which occurred very early in 169.[164] Marcus then no longer had a Verus to send to the East in case trouble again broke out. He felt, no doubt, that he must be fully relieved of Eastern affairs in order to carry on properly the war in the North.[165] It seems quite reasonable then to infer that soon after the death of Verus, Cassius was put in control in the East. We see him exercising this power in putting down a rebellion in Egypt in 172.[166]

In 175 Cassius revolted. It is now possible, with the help of the only dated document of his reign, to place his revolt a little

[157] See below p. 36 — and (1).
[158] See ref. under note 155; also Pt. 2, p. 92.
[159] E. Napp, De Rebus Imp. M. Aurel. Ant. p. 38ff. G. Wolffgramm, Des Avid. Cassius Stellung im Orient, Philol. XLII (1884), p. 186ff.
[160] Mommsen, R. G. V, p. 407. P.-W. III, 1844. Dodd, N. C. (1911), p. 259.
[161] P. A. E. S. III, A, 2, p. 91, 155. As this is the only inscription of Cassius found apparently in Arabia it may prove to be evidence not of his maius imperium, but for the assigning of Salkhad to Syria.
[162] XII, 2, D.
[163] Boissevain ed. of Dio, vol. III, p. 660 = Dio Cassius LXXI, 3, 1.
[164] Liebenam, Fasti p. 108.
[165] Schiller I, p. 647.
[166] P.-W. I, 2298.

earlier than has formerly been done.[167] The papyrus (5) is dated May 3, 175 in the first year of Avidius Cassius. Now Wilcken has shown,[168] from dates of papyri and ostraka, that the news of a change of emperors was often unknown for months in the inland cities of Egypt. On that evidence it is then safe to assume that Cassius had been recognized at Alexandria at least a month and a half earlier.[169] We may then date the beginning of the revolt in Syria late in March or early in April. According to Dio, the revolt of Cassius lasted three months and six days.[170] Hence it must have ended in all probability early in July. That this conclusion is true is made probable by the fact that we find Marcus Aurelius again recognized as emperor on a papyrus[171] from the Fayum, dated Aug. 23, 175.

P. Martius Verus 175-178

(1) I. G. R. III, 1290; Αὐτοκράτορσι Καίσ[αρσι Μ. Αὐρηλί]ῳ Ἀντωνείνωι κ[αὶ Λ. Αὐρηλίῳ Κομμόδῳ] Σεβ. τοῖς κυρίο[ις ἐπὶ Μαρτίου Οὐ]ήρου πρεσβ. Σεβ. ἀν[τιστρατήγου, ἐφεστῶτος] Πετουσίου Εὐδήμου. .... (il-Kefr.)

(2) I. G. R. III, 1195; ὑπὲρ σωτηρίας καὶ νίκης τῶν κυρίων Αὐτοκρατόρων Μ. Αὐρηλίου Ἀντωνείνου καὶ Λ. Αὐρηλίου [Κομμόδου] υἱοῦ αὐτοῦ Σεβ[α]στῶν, ἐπὶ Μαρτίου Οὐήρου πρέσβ. Σεβ. ἀντιστρ., ἐφεστῶτος Πετουσίου Εὐδήμου ἑκατοντάρχου λεγι. ις΄ Φλ. Φίρ. - - - (Schuhba).

Dio Cassius LXXI, 29, 2; λέγεται δὲ καὶ ὅτι Οὐῆρος ἐς τὴν Συρίαν, ἧς καὶ τὴν ἀρχὴν ἔλαβε, προπεμφθείς, καὶ εὑρὼν αὐτὰ (τὰ γράμματα) ἐν τοῖς σκεύεσι τοῦ Κασσίου ἠφάνισεν, εἰπὼν ὅτι μάλιστα μὲν ἐκείνῳ τοῦτ' ἔσται κεχαρισμένον, ἂν δὲ καὶ χαλεπήνῃ τι, ἄμεινόν γε ἔσται ἕνα ἑαυτὸν ἀντὶ πολλῶν ἀπολέσθαι.

[167] Schiller I, p. 657 ff., dates the end in the fall of 175. v. Arnim in P.-W. I, 2300, dates the beginning at the end of April or the first part of May. See Appendix, I, p. 94.

[168] Gk. Ostr. I, p. 800ff.

[169] There is an ostrakon from Thebes dated May 10, 175 under Marcus Aurelius; but this does not at all prevent the assignment of the revolt of Cassius to a date a month and a half earlier than his dated papyrus. See above, and n. 168.

[170] LXXI, 27.

[171] B. G. U. I, 127, l. 5. cf. no. 55, l. 21. The evidence from Fayum no. 332 is uncertain. See Appendix, II, p. 94.

Consul suff. in March, 166. Consul ord. II in 179.

Martius Verus was no doubt the successor of Cassius in Syria. The inscriptions (1), (2), to be sure, can hardly be placed earlier than 177, since Commodus is already Augustus;[172] but the passage in Dio (3) seems to me to fix Verus in 175. The finding and destroying of the letters of Cassius would naturally take place soon after Cassius' revolt, and not after the lapse of some years during which another governor was in power.[173] The view that Verus became governor in 175 is confirmed by a new inscription, dated in 175[174] of his successor in Cappadocia, C. Arrius Antoninus.[175] Verus was very probably retained in Syria through 178, for in 179 he was further rewarded, for his loyalty to the emperor during the revolt of Avidius Cassius,[176] by the consulship.

M. Pontius M. f. Pup. Laelianus Larcius Sabinus
178—Circa 180

(1) C. I. L. VI, 1497; M. Pontio M. f. Pup. Laeliano Larcio Sabino, cos., pontifici, sodali Antoniniano Veriano, fetiali, leg. Aug. pr. pr. prov. Syriae, leg. Aug. pr. pr. prov. Pannon. Super., leg. Aug. pr. pr. Pannon. Infer., comiti Divi Veri Aug., donato donis militarib. bello Armeniaco et Parthico ab Imp. Antonino Aug. et a Divo Vero Aug. etc.

(2) Fronto, ed. Naber p. 128, Lib. II, 1 ;—Milites Antiochiae adsidue plaudere histrionibus consueti, saepius in nemore vicinae ganeae quam sub signis habiti - - - adeo ut vir gravis et veteris disciplinae Laelianus Pontius loricas partim eorum digitis primoribus scinderet - - -

Consul ord. in 163.

Laelianus[177] was governor of Syria under Marcus Aurelius,

---

[172] Liebenam, Fasti p. 108.

[173] In I. G. R. III, 1195 and 1290, he is properly dated in 175. Liebenam p. 386, is surely mistaken in suggesting that the term of Pontius Laelianus comes between Cassius and Verus. Liebenam is followed by Brünnow Arabia III, p. 300, who makes a further mistake (p. 266, note) in stating that Martius Verus is only known from inscriptions.

[174] A. E .(1910), 161. Marcus Aurelius is entitled Germanicus on this stone; but not yet Sarmaticus, a title received in the course of 175. (Liebenam, Fasti p. 108.)

[175] On this man in general see Prosop. I, 139, 894.

[176] Dio Cassius LXXI, 23, 3ff.

[177] Ritterling, A. E. M. XX (1897), p. 22 ff., tries to show that the

very probably after the death of Verus as our inscription shows[178] (1). Probably at once, after holding the consulship, he went to the East as comes of Verus during the "bellum Armeniacum et Parthicum," 163-166.[179] It is to this period, no doubt, that Fronto refers (2). Now an allowance of only one year each for the Pannonian provinces,[180] would place his governorship of Syria not earlier than the middle of 168. Since however this brings him within the term of Avidius Cassius, it is necessary to put him[181] after Martius Verus, the immediate successor of Cassius. I have no hesitation in dating him as the successor of Verus, for he was surely governor before the death of Marcus Aurelius.[182]

P. Helvius Pertinax   Circa 180-182

(1) Vita Pertinacis 2, 10; Cassiano moto conposito e Syria ad Danuvii tutelam profectus est atque inde Moesiae utriusque, mox Daciae regimen accepit. Bene gestis his provinciis Syriam meruit.

(2) Op. cit. 3, 1; Integre se usque ad Syriae regimen Pertinax tenuit, post excessum vero Marci pecuniae studuit.

Consul suff. probably in 175.[183]

After the consulship he held the government of the two Moesias,[184] then of Dacia, and finally of Syria (1), before the

Laelianus of our inscription (1) is the governor of Pannonia Sup. in 148/149. He supports his claim by two incorrect assumptions; one, that our inscription is not chronologically arranged; the other, that the governors of Syria from 168 to the end of Marcus Aurelius' rule are all known, so that Laelianus must come before. Stout's view, Govs. of Moesia p. 52, is preferable.

[178] "Imp. Antoninus"; but "Divus Verus."

[179] See p. 33, under Avidius Cassius, also Schiller I, p. 640ff.

[180] Terms of governors under the Antonines were regularly long. Attidius Cornelianus and Avidius Cassius in Syria, Martius Verus in Cappadocia are good examples. (See also Vita Ant. Pii 5.)

[181] Liebenam (p. 386 and note), who incorrectly places this governor between Avidius Cassius and Martius Verus (see under Verus note 173) also suggests that he might have followed Iulius Verus; but this view is certainly incorrect if the explanation of the cursus in (1) be at all correct.

[182] The fact that Laelianus is called sodalis Antoninianus et Verianus, but not Marcianus, is also good evidence that he was back at Rome before the death of Marcus. Cf. Marq. St. V. III, p. 472.

[183] P.-W. V, 415.

[184] Stout, Govs. of Moesia p. 31. Liebenam p. 102ff.

38

death of Marcus Aurelius, if we may at all trust the evidence of the Vita (2). Prior to the time of Laelianus, who was back in Rome before the death of Marcus,[185] the governors are known for á considerable number of years. Again beginning with Dexter, there is probably an unbroken series. Between Laelianus and Dexter's known date there must be some three or four years. Here we should reasonably place Pertinax. He began his term then, as successor of Laelianus, probably late in 179 or early in 180. It is not likely that there was another governor between him and Dexter. We may then perhaps trust the evidence of the Vita,[186] which says that after his return from Syria he was obliged to live away from Rome for three years until the death of Perennis. This probably occurred in 185.[187] Pertinax may have governed therefore into the year 182. It seems quite probable that an inscription found at Hinè in Syria refers to his governorship.[188]

C. Domitius Dexter   Circa 182-183/184

Wadd. 2308 = I. G. R. III, 1276; ἔτους η′ κυρίου Καίσαρος Μ. [Κομόδου] Ἀντωνίνου, ἐπὶ Δομιττίου Δέξτρου ὑπατικοῦ, ἡ πόλις τοὺς ἀπὸ τῶν πηγῶν ἀγωγοὺς Ἄρρων, Καινάθων, Ἀφετάθων, Ὀρσούων, ἐπεσκεύασεν καὶ κατεσκεύασεν - - -. (Soada = Suwêdâ).

Consul suff. anno incert. before 183/184. Consul ord. in 196.

It seems best, with Brünnow,[189] to count the years of Commodus from the end of Nov. 176, when he was made co-regent by his father, on the evidence of an inscription,[190] dated in the sixteenth year of Commodus, which plainly is counted from that time. I do not, however, follow Brünnow in making the years of Commodus, on these inscriptions,[191] coincide with his tribunician powers. Now his trib. pot. I came to an end

---

[185] See p. 38, n. 182.
[186] Vita Pertinacis 3, 2-5.
[187] Prosop. III, 317, 146.
[188] I. G. R. III, 1096 (from Fossey, B. C. H. XXI (1897), p. 61 ff.). The editors of the I. G. R. have joined together inscriptions which were not even found at the same place. No doubt they were misled by the somewhat confusing arrangement in the B. C. H. pp. 61-63. This governor Pertinax is then by no means to be dated in 282/283.
[189] Arabia III, p. 320.
[190] Wadd. 2413 f = P. A. E. S. III, A, 5, 652. The same practice is seen in Wadd. 2455 dated in the eleventh year of Caracalla.
[191] For a list of inscriptions from this region, South Syria, see Brünnow, Arabia III, p. 267.

Dec. 10, 176,[192] though it only began Nov. 27; but I think it much more likely that his year 1 would be counted from the end of Nov. 176 to the same date 177, or, better still, to the beginning of the new year according to the calendar in use, as was the case at Alexandria in Egypt.[193] The new year in South Syria generally began,[194] since it was according to the calendar of Antioch, on October 1st in all probability.[195] The eighth year of Commodus would then begin on October 1st, 183. It seems very probable that Dexter[196] was the immediate successor of Pertinax.

Iulius Saturninus   Autumn 185/186

(1) Wadd. 2309 = I. G. R. III, 1277 ; ἔτους ι' [τοῦ ἡμῶν] κυρίου Αὐτοκράτορος [- - -][197], ὑπατεύοντος Ἰουλίου Σατορνείνου, ἡ πόλις τὸ κτίσμα σὺν ἐργαστηρίοις καὶ παντὶ κόσμῳ κα[τεσκεύασεν] - - -. (Soada = Suwêdâ).

(2) Wadd. 2524 = I. G. R. III, 1119 ; Ἰούλιος Σατουρνῖνος Φαινησίοις μητροκωμίᾳ τοῦ Τράχωνος χαίρειν - - (Phaena = il Mismîyeh).

(2) Brünnow, Arabia III, p. 203, 13 ; Γ. Πε[τ]ρώνιον Γ.... Σεκοῦνδον Βρονδ[.... λεγ.]δ' Σκυθ. πρινκιπα [..... ἡγεμονίας] Ἰουλ. Σατορνείνου [πρεσβ. Σεβ.] ἀντιστρ. Σειηνοὶ - - -. (Kanawât). Cf. A. A. E. S. III, no. 405.

(4) Wadd. 2309 a = C. I. G. 4618 ; Σα]τ[ο]ρνείνου ὑπ[ατι]κοῦ. (Same place as (1)).

Consul anno incert.

Waddington noted, in relation to the inscription (1), that of the emperors of the second and third centuries, whose names

[192] Liebenam, Fasti p. 109. C. I. L. III, D. 76. C. I. L. III, 3202; XIV, 3449. The same is shown with probability by C. I. L. II, 1725b; III, 14370[2]; IX, 5430.
[193] This same system for dating imperial years evidently held at Caesarea in Cappadocia, where there is found a coin of the nineteenth year of Septimius Severus (B. M. C. Galatia—(1899), p. 75, no. 232) showing that his year 1 must have run from spring to autumn of 193. Similarly for Galba, and Vespasian, see B. M. C. Phoenicia p. cxxxix; and Pick, Z. N. XIV (1887), p. 339.
[194] P.-W. I, 649. I. G. R. III, index pp. 664 and 665 for refs.
[195] See Prentice in P. A. E. S. III, B, 5, p. 138ff.; also Kubitschek, P.-W. I, 633. In the late empire the year began on Sep. 1. See Prentice, l. c.; also O. Kaestner, De Aeris p. 15.
[196] Possibly there is a reference to his early career in A. E. (1911), 145.
[197] The editors supply Severus Alexander.

are erased on the monuments, only two, Commodus and Severus Alexander, had a tenth year. He chose the latter[198] for this case. Brünnow however has proved[199] that Commodus must be the emperor, for in (3) this governor is connected with the Fourth Scythica legion, which was then in South Syria, where it did not belong at all after the division of the province by Septimius Severus. The Third Gallica alone belonged to the Southern part, Syria Phoenice.[200] It may be noted further that, though Syria Phoenice was a praetorian province,[201] in (1) Saturninus is termed ὑπατεύοντος,[202] a term which properly belongs to the legate of a consular province.

Dating this inscription on the same principles used for Domitius Dexter, we find Saturninus governor in the year beginning with autumn 185.

Asellius Aemilianus   Circa 186/190

(1) Wadd. 2213 = I. G. R. III, 1262; ὑπὲρ σωτηρίας καὶ νείκης κυρίου Κα[ίσα]ρος Κομόδου, ἐπὶ Ἀσελλίου Αἰμιλιαν[οῦ ὑ]πατικοῦ, ἐφεστῶτος Ἀγικίου Ῥωμανοῦ ἑκατοντάρχου? - - - ἔτους ι?

(2) Herodian III, 2, 3; οἱ μὲν γάρ (φασιν) φθονοῦντα (Αἰμιλιανὸν) τῷ Νίγρῳ ἐπιβουλεῦσαι, ἀγανακτοῦντα ὅτι δὴ διάδοχος αὐτοῦ γενόμενος τῆς ἐν Συρίᾳ ἀρχῆς ἔμελλεν ἔσεσθαι κρείττων.

(3) Z. N. XXIV (1904), p. 32; Αὐτ. Καις. Λ. Αὐρ. Κόμοδος | ἦγε. Ἀσελ. Αἰμιλιανοῦ Οὐλπίας Πανταλίας.

From a coin discovered in recent years (3) we learn that Aemilianus was governor of Thrace 176/180.[203] Since Thrace was a praetorian province,[204] his consulship must be dated between this period and that of his governorship of Syria.

Herodian (2) plainly states that Niger was the successor of Aemilianus, therefore Saturninus is not to be placed be-

---

[198] He is followed by the editors of I. G. R. III, 1277, and by Prentice, A .A. E. S. III; no. 405.

[199] Arabia III, p. 269.

[200] Domaszewski, Rangord. p. 179.

[201] See under Venidius Rufus p. 53, and The Division of Syria p. 87.

[202] For other instances of the use of this term for a consular governor see A. E. M. X (1886), p. 243, no. 11; op. cit. XVII (1894), p. 181; I. G. R. I, 591. So too of ὑπατικός (4) usually. See Brünnow, Arabia III, p. 281.

[203] H. Dressel, ed. of the coin, says that this period is certain from the type of the head of Commodus.

[204] Liebenam p. 389.

tween their terms of office, although Brünnow[205] has so placed him. Unfortunately all that can be learned from (1) with certainty is that Aemilianus was governor under Commodus. Waddington reads at the end ἔτους ιφ or ιρ which I can not explain.[206]

C. Pescennius Niger[207]   Circa 190-193

(1) Dio Cassius LXXIV, 6, 1 ; οὗτος δὲ (Νίγρος) Ἰταλὸς μὲν ἦν, ἐξ ἱππέων, οὔτε δὲ ἐς τὸ κρεῖττον οὔτε ἐς τὸ χεῖρον ἐπίσημος - - - · διὸ καὶ τῇ Συρίᾳ ὑπὸ Κομμόδου προσετάχθη.

(2) Vita Pesc. Nigri. 1, 5 ; Ordines (Niger) diu duxit multisque ducatibus pervenit, ut exercitus Syriacos iussu Commodi regeret, suffragio maxime athletae qui Commodum strangulavit, ut omnia tunc fiebant.

(3) Herodian II, 7, 4 ; ἦν δὲ ὁ Νίγρος τῶν μὲν πρὸ πολλοῦ ὑπα τεύσαντων, καθ᾽ ὃν δὲ καιρὸν τὰ προειρημένα ἐν Ῥώμῃ ἐπράττετο, Συρίας ἡγεῖτο πάσης. πολλὴ δὲ ἦν καὶ μεγίστη ἀρχὴ τότε, τοῦ τε Φοινίκων ἔθνους παντὸς καὶ τῆς μέχρις Εὐφράτου γῆς ὑπὸ τῇ Νίγρου ὄντων ἐξουσίᾳ.

According to the Vita[208] Niger was consul before Severus, who, as is learned from Dio,[209] was consul during the domination of Cleander. Now Cleander seems to have been killed in 189,[210] so that Niger must have held the consulship by 188 at the latest. But he was very probably consul some time before, and this probability is confirmed by the passage from Herodian (3).[211]

The date of the beginning of Niger's governorship in Syria is not known, but certainly he was in charge by the year 192, for Dio and the Vita (2) both state that he was appointed by Commodus.[212] Since he had affairs so well in hand that he was able to conduct a great revolt early in 193, the beginning of his term is probably to be set back as far as 190 or 191. Niger was defeated and killed by Severus late in 193.[213]

[205] Arabia III, p. 300.
[206] If it were possible to read ιβ or ιε, the years 187/188 or 190/191 respectively would be indicated.
[207] The "Iustus" added after "Niger," during his revolt, on coins and papyri is probably a title. Z. N. II (1875), p. 250, has it translated Δίκαιος . Cf. Eckhel III, 157.
[208] Vita Pesc. Nigri 4, 6.
[209] LXXII, 12.
[210] Prosop. I, 410, 883.
[211] Premerstein, Klio XIII (1913), p. 102, dates the consulship 180/183.
[212] Commodus was killed Dec. 31, 192. See Liebenam, Fasti p. 108.
[213] See below under The Revolt of Pescennius Niger, p. 78ff.

GOVERNORS OF SYRIA COELE

L. Alfenus Senecio 199

(1) C. I. L. III, 6709; Imp. Caes. L. Septimius Severus Pius Pertinax Aug. Arabic. Adiab. Parthic. Princeps Felic., Pontif. Max., Trib. Pot. XII, Imp. VIII, Cos. II, Procos., et Imp. Caes. M. Aurel. Antoninus Aug., Augusti n. fil., Procos., Imp. III, et P. Septimius [Ge]ta Caes., fil. et frater Augg. nn., pontem Chabinae fluvi a solo restituerunt et transitum reddiderunt, sub Alfenum Senecionem leg. Augg. pr. pr., curante Mario Perpetuo leg. Augg. leg. XVI F. F. (in ponte fluvii Bölam-Su). Cf. no. 6710, found on same bridge, and very similar to this inscription.

Consul suff. anno incert. before 199.

Satisfactory conclusions as to the date of these inscriptions can not be gained by a mere juggling of the figures;[1] but must be based on the fact that Caracalla is mentioned as Augustus. This shows that the date is 198 or later.[2] Now Marius Perpetuus, mentioned as legate of the Sixteenth Flavia, immediately after this office held the governorship of Arabia,[3] probably in the year 200.[4] The inscriptions of Senecio are then confined to 198, 199 or 200. The cos. II on them is therefore correct. Stout's suggestion,[5] that the tr. pot. XII is for tr. pot. VII, is quite plausible, and would give definitely 199 as the date. Imp. VIII seems quite beyond reasonable emendation; but it may be

---

[1] So the editors have done, and Stout, Govs. of Moesia p. 37, n. 74b.

[2] Liebenam, Fasti p. 110.

[3] C. I. L. III, 1178 contains his cursus.

[4] The inscription (C. I. L. III, 14150 = Brünnow, Arabia I, p. 21) of Perpetuus, when governor of Arabia, gives Severus' titles as tr. pot. VIII, Imp. XI, cos. III. To bring harmony among the figures, it seems better to emend to cos II, rather than to tr. pot. X. If consul III were correct we should expect cos. with Caracalla's name. Brünnow's suggestion (Arabia III, p. 290) of tr. pot. VIIII will not do, since this gives the year 201, while cos. III began in 202.

[5] See ref. in note 1.

worth while to note that this was the last imperatorship taken
by Severus before he left the East in 196 to oppose Albinus.[6]

Senecio was of course legate of Syria Coele,[7] since the inscriptions are from the extreme North of Syria. It is quite
possible that he was the first legate, although we do not know
how long before or after 199 he governed. He is known as
governor of Britain[8] between 205 and 208.[9]

[P. Cornelius Anullinus]

C. I. L. II, 5506 (a better reading of 2073) ;
P. Cornel. P. f. Gal. Anullino

— — — — — —

[leg] Aug. pr. pr. prov. . . . .
. . . . curat. — — — —

This inscription, of which only a part is here given, was
formerly read (no. 2073) - - leg] Aug. pr. pr[o]v
Sur[iae - - - - - .
On the basis of this reading Liebenam[10] of course included him
among the governors of Syria. Brünnow[11] followed him,
although the reading had been corrected in the meantime.

[L. Calpurnius]

The inscription[12] which represents this man as governor of
Syria Coele, is in all probability forged in part, as the editors
note. From the place where the stone was found it is evident that, if governor at all, he must have been governor of
Syria Phoenice, for which there is no proof whatever.

[6] A Wirt, Quaest. Sev. p. 10.
[7] The division of Syria was in 194. See p. 87ff.
[8] Domaszewski, Rangord., p. 180ff., shows that Britain was regularly
held by governors before Syria. (P. Helvius Pertinax is an exception.
See Prosop. I, 133, 49.) In the case of Senecio it is plain that after
the division of Syria, Britain ranks Syria Coele. So Germania Inf.
ranks Syria Phoenice (see under The Division of Syria, p. 90), while
it is still ranked by Syria Coele (C. I. L. VI, 1450).
[9] Liebenam p. 108.
[10] Die Leg. p. 387.
[11] Arabia III, pp. 300 and 321.
[12] C. I. L. III, 128.

L. Marius L. f. Quir. Maximus Perpetuus Aurelianus

202/209

C. I. L. VI, 1450; L. Mario L. f. Quir. Maximo Perpetuo Aureliano cos., sacerdoti fetiali, leg. Augg. pr. pr. provinc. Syriae Coelae, leg. Augg. pr. pr. provinc. Germaniae Inferioris item provinc. Belgicae, duci exerciti Mysiaci aput Byzantium et aput Lugdunum, leg. leg. I Italic. cur. viae Latinae - - - - M. Iulius Artemidorus leg. III Cyrenaicae.

Consul suff. anno incert. before circa 200. Consul II ord. in 223.

As the inscription shows, Marius Maximus fought at Byzantium, and then at Lugdunum against Albinus early in 197.[13] Since he cannot have been a provincial legate of Severus before this year, and since Valerius Pudens[14] preceded him as governor of Germania Inferior, probably his term in Germany began about 200, certainly not much before. After this office Maximus held the governorship of Syria Coele, undoubtedly after Alfenus Senecio. Probably his term did not begin before circa 202, if we allow him only two or three years in Germany. Since he was legate of the two Augusti only, he must be dated before 209, when Geta also became Augustus.[15] Possibly the dedication by an officer of the third Cyrenaica should be dated during the term of Marius Perpetuus in Arabia, who may have been the brother of Marius Maximus.

[Alfenus Avitianus]

This man, mentioned as governor in an inscription[16] from Gerasa, was, as Brünnow[17] has rightly shown, governor of Arabia.

Fabius Agrippinus

217/218

Dio Cassius LXXIX, 3, 4; ἐφόνευσε μὲν γὰρ ἐν τῇ Συρίᾳ τόν τε Νέστορα καὶ Φάβιον Ἀγριππῖνον τὸν ἄρχοντα αὐτῆς, τῶν τε ἱππέων τῶν ἀμφὶ τὸν Μακρῖνον τοὺς πρώτους.

---

[13] Schiller I, p. 716ff.
[14] Liebenam p. 200.
[15] Liebenam, Fasti p. 110.
[16] I. G. R. III, 1371.
[17] Arabia III, pp. 269 and 298, where Brünnow has apparently forgotten that Syria was divided before this time.

Consul suff. anno incert.

Agrippinus was governor, under Macrinus, of Syria Coele evidently since we have a governor of Phoenice for this same time.[18] I can see no occasion for Liebenam's note[19] which represents him as governor of Syria Phoenice.

Q. Atrius Clonius   Circa 222

(1) C. I. L. II, 4111; Q. Atrio Clonio leg. Aug. pr. pr. provinciarum Thraciae, Cappadociae, Syriae Maioris, Hispaniae Citerioris, Claudius Iustus 7 leg. VII Gem. P. F. Severianae Alexandrianae praesidi abstinentissimo. (Tarraco, Spain.)

(2) I. G. R. I, 717; Ἀγαθῇ τύχῃ ὑπὲρ ὑγείας καὶ νείκης Μ. Αὐρ. Ἀντωνείνου κατὰ κελευσιν τοῦ λαμπρότατου ὑπατικοῦ Κ. Ἀτρίου Κλονίου τέχνης, Βυ[ρ]σ[έων —. (Thrace)

(3) Dig. XXVI, 10, 7, 2;—ex epitula imperatoris nostri et divi Severi ad Atrium Clonium.

Consul suff. anno incert. circa 212.

The form of the inscription (1) shows plainly that it was set up during the governor's term in the province. The order of the province held is then the ascending. The position of Thrace, undoubtedly a praetorian province under Septimius Severus and later,[20] points to the same conclusion. Furthermore, while (1) is plainly of the reign of Severus Alexander,[21] the inscription (2) of Clonius in Thrace, is evidently of the reign of Caracalla, so that it is again clear that (1) is in the ascending order. Domaszewski is therefore wrong in giving the order of the provinces, Hispania Citerior, Syria Maior, Cappadocia.[22]

Now if the passage from the Digest (3) may be connected with Clonius' cursus, we can date his Thracian governorship with approximate accuracy. Inscription (2) is from the reign of Caracalla; (3) is of Severus and Caracalla. Hence we date Clonius in Thrace at the end of Severus' reign, and the be-

[18] Dio Cassius LXXVÍII, 35, 1.
[19] Die Leg. p. 388, n. 1. Brunnow, Arabia III, p. 301, rightly considers him governor of Syria Coele.
[20] A. E. (1892), 9; (1900), 19; (1907), 45.
[21] Note the titles of the legion.
[22] Rangord. p. 181. The ref. (note 5) is incorrect, for surely C. I. L. II, 4111 was intended.

ginning of Caracalla's.[23] Since he is called ὑπατικός (2), no doubt he gained the consulship while in the province.[24] Then followed his Cappadocian and Syrian governorships. The Syria Maior can, of course, only refer to Syria Coele. The Spanish governorship fell in the time of Alexander Severus. It seems best to put the term in Syria after that of Fabius Agrippinus. It would not be likely that the three commands of Thrace, Cappadocia, and Syria would be crowded in between 212 and 217, with the Spanish coming after 222. I would date his Syrian command roughly at about the beginning of Severus Alexander's reign.

D. Simonius Proculus Iulianus   239/252

C. I. L. VI, 1520; [D. S]imoni Proculi Iuliani c. [v. . . . . prov. Sy]riae Coeles, Daciarum III P[. . . . iur]idico per Transpadum. Pr[. . . . . .

Julianus was legate of Thrace under Maximinus;[25] then, under the same emperor, governor of Arabia[26] and consul designate. He must have been consul therefore circa 238. We know that he was praefectus urbi;[27] but the date at which he held this office is not at all certain. The only expression of time in any sense "Nobilissimus Caesar"[28] can not help here, for it is very general, as a glance at the list of emperors in the index of C. I. L. III will show. It is clear however that it was after 238, but before 254, for in this year begins the list of praefecti,[29] and Julianus does not appear on it. In this same period, and probably before the prefecture[30] are to be placed the Dacian[31] and Syrian governorships in order. The

---

[23] Kalopothakes, De Thracia p. 57, places him "sub Severo."
[24] See, for similar cases, Brünnow, Arabia III, p. 288.
[25] I. G. R. I, 692.
[26] Brünnow Arabia III, p. 292. Brünnow is certainly mistaken in placing Simonius Julianus before Pomponius. The fact that Simonius was legate in Thrace under Maximinus shows that his term in Arabia under the same emperor must fall in the last half of Maximinus' reign.
[27] C. I. L. XV, 7528. Orelli 4347 = Borghesi IX, p. 370.
[28] Orelli 4347.
[29] Mommsen ed. in Abh. Sächs. Ges. d. Wiss. I (1850), p. 627.
[30] Cf. Ch. Huelsen, M. R. I. xxi (1906), p. 88. The earlier rule, that the prefecture of the city was held last, was however not strictly kept in the later period. See Daremberg-Saglio s. v. praefectus urbi.
[31] C. I. L. III, 1573.

Syrian governorship then can hardly have been held before
239, or after 252.

Virius Lupus   Before 278

(1) C. I. L. VI, 31775; [Viri]o Lupo c. m. v. [cos. ord.]
praef. urbi. pontif. D. S., [iudici s]acrarum [co]gnition. [per
Aeg.] et per Ori[en]tem, praes. [Syriae] Coeles et Arabiae.
(2) Laterculus of 354 in Abh. Sächs. Ges. d. Wiss. (1)
1850, p. 627; (Cos.) Probo et Lupo (278) Virius Lupus
praefectus urbis; (Cos.) Probo III et Paterno (279) Virius
Lupus praefectus urbis; (Cos.) Messala et Grato (280) Virius
Lupus praefectus urbis.

The identification of the Lupus, governor of Syria Coele
(1), with the consul of 278 who was also prefect of the city
278-280 (2), seems to me certain.[32] By comparing the career
of Helvius Dionysius,[33] governor of Syria Coele under Diocletian, with that of Lupus, C. W. Keyes[34] concludes that
Lupus was governor before his consulship. This conclusion,
I believe, is correct; but I do not think that it should be based
on the cursus of Dionysius.[35] If the inscription (1) is in
proper chronological order, that order is evidently the descending, for Arabia was always held before the consulship, and
before the governorship of Syria Coele. It would seem clear
then that Lupus was governor of Syria also before his consulship. Furthermore a table of the governors of Arabia,
given by Keyes,[36] shows that, with the possible exception of
Lupus, all the governors known from 262 to the time of Diocletian were of equestrian rank. It seems very probable therefore that Lupus, who was of course of senatorial rank, was
governor of Arabia before 262. If this is so, it seems highly
improbable that Lupus held the governorship in Syria after
his consulship and prefecture of the city, i.e. after 280. Lupus
was then apparently a praetorian governor of Syria Coele.
He is the first and only governor whom we can, with a fair
degree of certainty, place in this class. The evidence to be
had does not show whether the change was permanent or not.

[32] See C. W. Keyes, The Rise of the Equites, Princeton, 1915, p. 16.
[33] C. I. L. VI, 1673. See below, p. 51.
[34] Op. cit. p. 17.
[35] See, for discussion, p 51.
[36] Op. cit. pp. 8-9.

(1) Zonaras XII, 28 ; Μαξιμῖνον δέ τινα συγγενῆ ἑαυτοῦ ἡγεμόνα τῆς Συρίας προεχειρίσατο Τάκιτος· ὁ δὲ κακῶς τῇ ἀρχῇ χρώμενος ἀνῃρέθη παρὰ στρατιωτῶν.

(2) Zosimus I, 63, 2; Μαξιμίνῳ γένει προσήκοντι τὴν Συρίας ἀρχὴν παραδέδωκεν. οὗτος τοῖς ἐν τέλει τραχύτατα προσφερόμενος εἰς φθόνον ἅμα καὶ φόβον κατέστησεν.

The references give Maximinus as governor of Syria under Tacitus.[37] Syria, of course, means Syria Coele.[38]

?Saturninus 276/282

(1) Zosimus I, 66, 1 ; ταῦτα διαπραξαμένῳ τῷ Πρόβῳ Σατουρνῖνος γένει Μαυρούσιος, ἐπιτήδειος ὢν ἐς τὰ μάλιστα τῷ βασιλεῖ διὰ τοῦτό τε καὶ τὴν Συρίας ἀρχὴν ἐπιτετραμμένος, τῆς βασιλέως ἀποστὰς πίστεως εἰς ἐπαναστάσεως ἔννοιαν ἦλθεν.

(2) Hieron. Chron., p. 184, ed. Schoene-Peterman = Sync. 723, 7 ; τῷ ϛʹ ἔτει Πρόβου Σατορνῖνος στρατοπεδάρχης τὴν καινὴν Ἀντιόχειαν ἤρξατο κτίζειν, ὃς ὕστερον ἐπαναστὰς τῇ Ῥωμαίων ἀρχῇ ἐσφάγη ἐν Ἀπαμείᾳ ὑπὸ τῶν ἰδίων.

(3) Op cit. p. 185 (Hieronymus) ; Anno Abr. 2297; Probus, anno 4 ; Saturninus magister exercitus novam civitatem Antiochiae orsus condere. Qui postea imperium molitus invadere Apamiae occiditur.

It is stated by Aurelius Victor,[39] Eutropius,[40] and Orosius,[41] that Saturninus revolted in the Orient, under Probus. Zonaras[42] simply cites him as a pretender in that reign. Zosimus (1) however says that he held the government of Syria,[43] and this statement is perhaps supported by the evidence of Syncellus (2) and Hieronymus (3) that Saturninus tried to found either a new city Antioch, or a new state at Antioch; but was killed at Apamea. Now according to the Vita Saturnini he held the office of dux limitis Orientalis,[44] under Aurelian, and

---

[37] Tacitus was emperor from the fall of 275 to the spring of 276. See Liebenam, Fasti p. 116.
[38] See, for example, Zosimus I, 64, 1 and Zonaras XII, 29.
[39] de Caes. 37, 3; Epit. 37, 2.
[40] IX, 17.
[41] Hist. VII, 24, 3.
[42] XII, 29.
[43] Jones, Hist. of Rom. Emp. p. 349.
[44] See J. H. E. Crees, Reign of Probus p. 114.

was first proclaimed emperor at Alexandria. If it be true that Saturninus had the right to visit Egypt in the discharge of his duties, he must of course have held some sort of general authority over the Orient, perhaps similar to that of Avidius Cassius. Vopiscus however is the only writer who tells this story, and his rhetorical account is suspicious.[45] According to the arrangement of the material in Zosimus, Saturninus' revolt falls rather early in Probus' reign. So Crees[46] prefers a date around 277. But Syncellus (2) gives the sixth year of Probus, which will agree with the year of Abraham 2297; but not with the fourth year of Probus, given by Hieronymus (3). Syncellus' dating, 281/2 A.D., is accepted by Domaszewski.[47]

Charisius   May 10, 290

Codex Just. IX, 41, 9; Idem AA. (Diocletianus et Maximianus) ad Charisium praesidem Syriae. - - - D. VI. id. Mai. Hemesa, ipsis IIII et III AA. conss.

Charisius was governor of Syria Coele under Diocletian. We know nothing more about him.

Primosus   293

Codex Just. VII, 33, 6; Pars epistulae Diocletiani et Maximiani AA. et CC. ad Primosum praesidem Syriae - - - accepta.

Primosus was governor of Syria Coele under Diocletian. The date is not definitely fixed; but the editors put it as 293, since this passage occurs among a number of others of that year.

Verinus   Sep. 22, 294

Codex Just. II, 12, 20; Idem AA. et CC. (Diocletianus et Maximianus) ad Verinum praesidem Syriae. - - - D. X k. Oct. Demesso. CC. conss.

Verinus was evidently governor of Syria Coele under Diocletian.

[45] Peter, Gesch, Litt. röm. Kzeit II, p. 339, says that Vopiscus has little historical value. Schiller I, p. 880, apparently accepts the story of Vopiscus.
[46] Op. cit. p. 158.
[47] G. R. K. II, p. 318.

50

L. Aelius Helvius Dionysius[48]   295 or 296

C. I. L. VI, 1673; L. Aelio Helvio Dionysio c. v. iudici sacrarum cognitionum totius Orien., praesidi Syriae Coele., correctori utriusq(ue) Italiae, curatori Aq. et Miniciae, curat. . . . . operum publicoru[m], pontifici dei Sol. . . . . collegium fabrorum tignuar. multis in se patrociniis co.

The title c. v. in the inscription shows that Dionysius was a governor of the senatorial order. He held the position of curator operum publicorum after 286.[49] He was curator Aq. et Miniciae very probably before 293.[50] Then, possibly in the same period, he had the position of corrector utriusque Italiae, from which he went to Syria Coele.

Now Dionysius was probably proconsul of Africa in 298,[51] and an inscription[52] of his term, shows that he held the position for four years. His prefecture of the city falls exactly in 301.[53] Hence it is plain, from Pallu de Lessert,[54] that the four years, in all probability, were 297-300 inclusive. Before this he held the governorship of Syria. Since he served in at least three positions after 286, it seems probable that he follows in Syria the governors given by the Codex. His term should be dated then with probability in 295 or 296.

The consulship of Dionysius is not mentioned in the inscription, and therefore it is natural to conclude that he had been governor of Syria before he held the consulship, as in the case of Virius Lupus.[55]. It is however to be noted that Dionysius, before his term in Syria, held the position of curator Aq. et Miniciae, which was regularly held by consulars during the

---

[48] For his cursus see P.-W. V, 914, no. 82; and Pallu de Lessert, Fastes Prov. Afr. II, p. 8.

[49] C. I. L. VI, 255 and 256. The date is sure from the fact that both the emperors Diocletian and Maximian appear in the inscriptions. Cf. Liebenam, Fasti p. 118.

[50] C. I. L. VI, 773. The emperors' names head the inscription; but no Caesars appear. Cf. Liebenam, Fasti p. 118.

[51] Jurisp. ante Just. p. 730 = Frag. Vat. 41.

[52] C. I. L. VIII, 12459.

[53] Laterculus of 254 in Abh. Sächs. Ges. d. Wiss. I (1850), p. 628.

[54] Op. cit. His list shows other governors for 294-5, and with probability for 295-6.

[55] See p. 48.

second and third centuries,[56] and probably during the reign of Diocletian.[57] This evidence would make it seem probable that Dionysius was a consular governor of Syria. It does not seem possible to decide the question with certainty.

[56] See P.-W. IV, 1784.
[57] See C. I. L. VI, 1418, and 31378. In these cases the office was very probably held after the consulship.

GOVERNORS OF SYRIA PHOENICE

Q. Venidius Rufus   194-198

Mél. Fac. Or. IV (1910), p. 216 = A. E. (1910), 106; [Imp.] Caesar L. Septimius Severus Pertinax Aug., Pontif. Max., Trib. Pot., Imp. III, Cos. II, P. P., vias et milia(ria) [per Q. Ve]nidium [R]u[fum l]eg. [A]ug. p[r.] p[r. (restituit?)]. (Near Zahleh).

(2) C. I. L. III, 6725; Imp. Caes. L. Septimio Severo Pio Pertinaci A[ug.] Arabico Adiabenico Parthico Maximo, P. M., Trib. Pot. VI, Imp. XI, [c]os. II., P. P., Procos., et Imp. Caes. M. Aurelio Antonino Aug., Trib. Pot., fil. eius. şub Ven[i]dio Ru[f]o leg. Augg. pr. pr. XVIII E ΜΑΛΕ. (three hours and one mile N. W. of Palmyra). Cf. 6723, very similar.

(3) C. I. L. III, 205; Imperatores Caesares, L. Septimius Severus Pius Pertinax Aug. Arabicus Adeabenicus Parthicus Maximus, Tribuniciae Potes. VI, Imp. XI, cos. II, Procos., P. P., et M. Aurel. Antoninus Aug., filius eius, vias et miliaria per Q. Venidium Rufum leg. Augg. pr. pr., praesidem provinc. Syriae Phoenic. renovaverunt. II, B. (Near Sidon).

For other inscriptions very similar, see under this same number.

Rufus was the first governor of Syria Phoenice and held office from the year 194[1] to about 198, (2) and (3). He was not of the consular, but of praetorian rank.[2]

−ητιανος   208/209

I. G. R. III, 1149; ὑπὲρ σωτηρίας τῶν κυρίων Λ. Σεπ. Σεουήρου καὶ Ἀντωνείνου κ[αὶ Γέτα] ὑῶν αὐτοῦ καὶ Ἰου(λίας) Δό[μ]ν[ης] Σεβ., ἔτους ιϛ′, [ἐπὶ .....]ητιανοῦ[3] [πρεσβ.] Σεββ. [ἀν]τ[ιστρ(ατήγου), ἡ κώμη ἀν]έσ[τη]σεν διὰ [Αὔ]σου Λαν .... (Harran).

[1] On the dating of (1) see under The Division of Syria, p. 87.

[2] See The Division of Syria, p. 87. Rufus gives us another example of a praetorian going from a province without a legion to one with a legion—Cilicia to Syria Phoenice. (Cf. Domaszewski, Rangord, p. 174)

[3] The editors supply [Αὐρ]η[λ]ιανοῦ; but Wetzstein's copy in Abh. d.

Harran, where this inscription of a governor was found, was very probably within Syrian territory.[4] The governor therefore must be of Syria Phoenice. It can not be assigned to Marius Maximus,[5] as the editors of I. G. R. propose to do, since the provinces are not the same. Nor can it belong to Alfenus Avitianus, as Brünnow[6] suggests, for if he was governor of one of the Syrias at all, he must be assigned to Syria Coele. Naturally the inscription can only honor the governor of the province to which the locality, in which it is found, belongs. It is dated in the seventeenth year of Severus, i.e. 208/209 A.D., if we reckon Severus' first year from the spring of 193 to the beginning of the year at Antioch in the autumn of the same year.[7]

D. Pius Cassius   Dec. 10, 212/213

C. I. L. III, 202 and p. 973; [Imp. Ca]es[a]ri Divi [L. Sep]t[im]i S[e]ve[r]i Pi[i] [Pert. Aug. A]rabici Adiabenici Par[thici] Max. Brit. [Ma]x. [fil.], Divi Marci Antonini Pii [Ge]rmanici Sar[mati]ci nepoti, Divi Antonini Pii pronep., Divi Hadriani ab[n]epo[t.] - - - M. [A]u[relio] Antonino Pio Aug. Part[h Max., P]at[ri] Pat[r.], [Brit.] Max., [P]on[tific.] Maximo, Trib. Pot. XVI, Cos. [II]II, P[r]ocos., vias et miliari[a] per D. Pium Cassium leg. Aug. p[r.] p[r.] praesidem provinciae Syriae Phoenices, colonia Iulia Aug. [f]el. Hel. [r]en[o]v[a]vit.

The reading trib. pot. XVI (of Caracalla) seems good, hence this governor is dated in 213.[8] This is all we know of him.

Marius Secundus   217/218

Dio Cassius LXXVIII, 35, 1; διῆγεν δέ τινα καὶ Μάριος Σεκοῦνδος, καίπερ βουλευτής τε ὑπὸ τοῦ Μακρίνου γεγονὼς καὶ τῆς Φοινίκης προστατῶν.

Akad. zu Berlin (1863), p. 296, no. 109, has plainly—ητιανου only. So too Wadd. 2460.
[4] Brünnow, Arabia III, p. 269. Cf. under Pomponious Julianus, p. 56.
[5] Governor of Syria Coele 202/209. See p. 45.
[6] Arabia III, p. 298, 5.
[7] Cf. under Domitius Dexter, p. 40.
[8] Caracalla's first trib. pot. extended from fall of 198 to Dec. 9; 198. Liebenam, Fasti p. 110.

Secundus was governor of Phoenice under Macrinus, that is in 217/218.[9]

Verus   218-circa 219

Dio Cassius LXXIX, 7, 1; ....ς .δὲ Οὐῆρος ἐπιτολμήσας καὶ αὐτὸς τῇ μοναρχίᾳ ἐν τῷ τρίτῳ στρατοπέδῳ τῷ Γαλλικῷ, οὗ ἦρχε, καὶ Γέλλιος Μάξιμος - - - ἐδικαιώθησαν.

As commander of the Third Gallica Verus was the legate of the province, according to the principle of government stated by Domaszewski,[10] that in a praetorian province the legate of the legion was the governor.[11] Verus governed early in the reign of Elagabalus,[12] in 219 probably, no doubt as the successor of Marius Secundus.

? Rutilius Pudens Crispinus   Circa 230

I. G. R. III, 1033; ἡ βουλὴ καὶ ὁ δῆμος Ἰούλιον Αὐρήλιον Ζηνόβιον - - στρατηγήσαντα ἐν ἐπιδημίᾳ θεοῦ Ἀλεξάνδρου, καὶ ὑπηρετήσαντα παρουσίᾳ διηνεκεῖ Ῥουτιλλίου Κρισπείνου τοῦ ἡγησαμένου καὶ ταῖς ἐπιδημησάσαις οὐηξιλλατίοσιν - - - - - - ἔτους δνφ'. (Palmyra).

Crispinus was governor of Thrace in the last part of Elagabalus' reign, and early in the reign of Severus Alexander.[13] Now according to the inscription he commanded troops at Palmyra, probably during the Persian war, circa 231-233.[14] He surely would not be a subordinate of the Phoenician governor, after being governor of Thrace. Hence he was either extraordinary commander of troops during the war, or legate of Syria Phoenice. The length of time between his term in Thrace and his position in Syria would tend to show that he was probably not governor, but commander in the war. A rescript of Severus Alexander,[15] dated August 229, and addressed Crispino, may perhaps refer to this man.

[9] Liebenam, Fasti p. 111.
[10] Rangord. p. 173.
[11] Good examples are given by C. I. L. III, 550 (of Hadrian), and C. I. L. X, 6321, with Dessau 1036 (of Q. Pompeius Falco).
[12] See Boissevain ed. of Dio vol. III, p. 460. Prosop. III, 406, 292.
[13] I. G. R. I, 669, 688, 772, 1472. In I. G. R. I, 718, Iulia Bassiana should no doubt be supplied and not Domna, as editors admit that Domna's name does not fill the space. A. E. (1900), 20 = I. G. R. I, 719, must be dated in the reign of Elagabalus, as Dobrusky supplies the name. There is not room enough for Severus Alexander's name.
[14] Schiller I, p. 780ff. Hopkins, Alex. Sev. p. 234ff.
[15] Codex Just. V, 62, 10. Cf. Prosop. III, 147, 166.

Wadd. 2399 = I. G. R. III, 1213; ὑπὲρ σωτηρίας καὶ νείκης καὶ
αἰωνίου διαμονῆς [τῶν κυρίων] ἡμῶν [Αὐτοκρατόρων Καισάρων Γ. Ἰουλ.
Μαξιμείνου καὶ Γ. Ἰουλ. Μαξίμου τοῦ] υἱοῦ αὐτοῦ Σεββ., ἐπὶ Πομπωνίου
Ἰουλιανοῦ πρεσβ. Σεββ. ἀντιστρ. ὑπατείας [Μαξιμείνου] καὶ Ἀφρι-
κανοῦ[16] - - - (Kafr il-Lehâ).

This inscription was found at Kafr il-Lehâ near Dêr il-
Leben, a territory which can be claimed for either Arabia or
Syria Phoenice. A line drawn from Kanawât through Atil
and Kerak to Der'ât will form the northernmost boundary of
territory that can with certainty be assigned to Arabia.[17] For
Syria Phoenice a southern boundary, beyond which is doubtful
territory, may reasonably be placed in a line drawn through il-
Hit and Lubbên (Agraena), based on the use of imperial years
in dating.[18] An inscription of the Third Gallica,[19] found at
Ezr'a (Zorava), is good evidence that the boundary lay as
far south as that place.

So then the inscription of Pomponius Julianus is located in
doubtful territory. Chronological considerations alone can
help us here. In the first place, it is dated by the consuls of
the year, though the method of dating inscriptions in Arabia
was by the era of Bostra.[20] Again, Pomponius is definitely dated
in the year 236. Now Simonius Julianus, who was governor of
Thrace under Maximinus, and then governor of Arabia also
under Maximinus, must have held the latter position hardly
earlier than the middle of that reign.[21] Hence he too is to be

[16] Consuls ord. in 236.
[17] See the evidence in Brünnow, Arabia III, p. 268, and especially
p. 269. He claims Philippopolis for Arabia on the evidence of Aurelius Victor, De Caesaribus c. 28. The region circa 175 belonged to
Syria (I. G. R. III, 1195). It may be that Philip, when he founded the
city some years later than the term of Julianus, changed the borders.
[18] Brünnow, l. c.
[19] Wadd. 2486 = I. G. R. III, 1157. The names of the sons of the
officer are barbarian; and the letter forms not early. The "III
Gallica" is not erased; hence the inscription is probably of the period
after the restoration of the legion. (See Daremberg-Saglio s. v. III
Gallica.)
[20] Brünnow, Arabia III, p. 267, and table. As a good example,
A. J. A. X (1906), p. 289.
[21] Brünnow, Arabia III, p. 293, admits that it is strange that Arabia
should have had two governors in the short reign of Maximinus; but
the fact is stranger than he states it, for he incorrectly thought that

dated circa 236 or 237. It is hardly fair to assume that Simonius is to be dated at the very end of Maximinus' reign. That would make his term very short indeed. In the years 238[22] and 239,[23] Domitius Valerianus is fixed as governor of Arabia, to be sure under another emperor.

The two governors then, Pomponius and Simonius, are dated very nearly at the same time. The probability therefore, it seems to me is that Pomponius was governor not of Arabia, but of the neighboring province, Syria Phoenice. This conclusion of course forces us to place Kafr il-Lehâ in Syria Phoenice at this time. If then Schuhba (later Philippopolis)[24] is rightly claimed for Arabia, the boundary line must have turned quite sharply southwest from that neighborhood, and skirted the Djebel-Hauran.

? -τος (or -γος)?   244/249

Wadd. 2076 = I. G. R. III, 1200; Θεῷ Μαρείνῳ .... τος ὑπα-[τικός]. (Schuhba = Philippopolis).

The inscription as edited, seems to have been set up by a governor. Unfortunately the letters after υπα are lost, so that it is not certain that the word was ὑπατικός; perhaps it was Ὑπα[τίου],[25] a patronymic. Since it concerns Marinus, father of the emperor Philip, it must have been set up between 244 and 249.[26] Now if this inscription refers to a governor,[27] it seems more likely that he was governor of Arabia, for Philippopolis was founded in Arabia, according to Aurelius Victor,[28] by Philip at the beginning of his reign. The popular cognomen

Simonius could be placed at the very beginning of the reign, in Arabia. See under Simonius Julianus in Syria Coele, p. 47. That the governorship of Arabia, with a legion, would follow that of Thrace, without a legion, is sure. See Domaszewski, Rangord. p. 173.

[22] A. J. A. X (1906), p. 289ff. = A. E. (1907), 67; year 133. This inscription, from Irbid, also fixes the boundary of Arabia definitely further west and north than Brünnow placed it. (Arabia III, p. 264ff.)

[23] Brünnow, Arabia III, p. 293; year 134.

[24] See above n. 17.

[25] Cf. Wadd. 2018.

[26] Prosop. II, 199, 272.

[27] The editors (I. G. R.) note, on the word ὑπατικός; "Legati Syriae iam secundo saeculo consulares vocabantur." This note is meaningless, for Syria had long been divided, and our inscription can only be of the smaller part, Syria Phoenice, if it belongs to Syria at all.

[28] De Caesaribus c. 28. See under Pomponius Julianus, n. 17.

Arabs, given to Philip, showing apparently that he was a native of Arabia, may tend to support the view that the city he founded was in his home province.

? L. Iulius Aurel. Sulp. Uranius[29] Antonius?   253/254

(1) B. M. C. Galatia- (1899), p. 240, 22 ; Αὐτοκ. Κ. Σουλπ. Ἀντωνῖνος Σεβ. | Δημαρχ. ἐξουσίας. S. C. EMICA.

(2) Hunt. Coll. III (1905), p. 198, 18; Αὐτοκ. Σουλπ. Ἀντωνῖνος Σε[β.] .... κολων. εξφ.

It is possible that this pretender at Emesa (1), in Syria Phoenice, 253/254 A.D. (2),[30] was governor of the province. His revolt seems to have been purely local.[31]

? Rufinus   253/257?

Anon. continuator Dionis in Müller, F. H. G. IV, p. 195, 7 ; ὅτι τὸν Ὀδέναθον τὸν παλαιὸν Ῥουφῖνος ἀναιρεῖ ὡς νεωτέροις ἐπιχειροῦντα πράγμασιν. Κατηγόρει δὲ ὁ νεώτερος Ὀδέναθος Ῥουφίνου ὡς φονεύσαντος τὸν πατέρα αὐτοῦ. ------- καὶ ἐπῄνεσε τοὺς λόγους αὐτοῦ (Ῥουφί-
νου) ὁ Γαλλιηνός.

Since Rufinus is here found exercising great authority, the position which he probably held, is that of governor[32] of Syria Phoenice, in which Palmyra was situated.[33]   It is of course possible that he was an extraordinary commander. The incident, as it is given, must be dated some time before early 258, when Odaenathus, the son, was in power,[34] and after 253, the beginning of Gallienus' reign.[35]   It is strange that we find Gallienus concerned in this story, for Valerian held complete control in the East until 260,[36] and so naturally the case would have been brought before him.   Perhaps, if the event took place during the joint reign of Valerian and Gallienus, the name of the latter, who held the stage for eight years[37] after Valerian's capture, was used by mistake.

---

[29] Prosop. II, 170, 125.

[30] On the era of Emesa, see Head, Hist. Num. p. 780.

[31] B. M. C. Galatia—(1899), p. 231, would attribute one of his coins to Antioch; but on slight grounds.

[32] Wadd. 2600, and notes.

[33] See under The Division of Syria, p. 88, n. 14.

[34] I. G. R. III, 1031.

[35] Liebenam, Fasti p. 115.

[36] Schiller I, p. 812ff. Liebenam, Fasti p. 114.

[37] Liebenam, *op. cit.* p. 115.

The matter would be clearer if we could connect father and son of this story with the men known from inscriptions; but this is not easily done. Waddington identified the elder Odaenathus with an Odaenathus who died before 251, and considered the younger Odaenathus a brother of Haeranes mentioned in an inscription.[38] He thus does violence to the story of Rufinus, dating it earlier. Mommsen[39] on the other hand supposed Haeranes of the inscription to have been the father of the great Odaenathus, and the grandson of the one who died before 251. This leaves a very short interval for the grandson to rise to great power by 258.[40]

?Septimius Odaenathus   April, 258

Wadd. 2602 = I. G. R. III, 1031 ; Σεπ[τίμιον 'Οδαίναθον] τὸν λαμπ[ρότατον ὑπατικ]ὸν[41]. συντέ[λεια τῶν χρυσοχ]όων καὶ ἀργ[υροκόπων τ]ὸν δεσπότην, τειμῆς χάριν, [ἔτ]ους θξφ', μηνει Ξανδικῷ[42]. (Palmyra).

The title ὁ λαμπρότατος ὑπατικὸς was sometimes used in Syria to denote the governor.[43] It is then possible that this inscription, found in Syria Phoenice, may refer to a governor of that province, for the title is also used of governors of praetorian provinces fairly frequently.[44] It is however to be noticed that other great men of the same family of Palmyra were given the honorary title λαμπρότατος συνκλητικός,[45] and it may be therefore that Odaenathus' title in this inscription is also an honorary one of higher degree. Schiller[46] does not agree with Waddington's[47] view that Odaenathus can have been governor; but since so little is known of his history at this time, at least the possibility that he was governor should be admitted.

[38] Wadd. 2600.
[39] R. G. V, 427.
[40] I. G. R. III, 1031.
[41] Supplied from the Palmyrene version, de Vogué, Inscr. Palmyr. no. 23.
[42] April, 258 A.D.; Seleucid era.
[43] I. G. R. III, 1179 and 1261.
[44] A. E. (1902), 134, a governor of Thrace; A. J. A. X (1906), p. 291, a governor of Arabia in 238, with exactly this title.
[45] I. G. R. III, 1034 and 1035.
[46] Vol. I, p. 825.
[47] No. 2602.

Codex Just. I, 23, 3; Impp. Diocletianus et Maximianus AA. Crispino praesidi, provinciae Phoenice. - - - D. prid k. April. Hannibaliano et Asclepiodoto conss. (292).

References possibly to the same man as governor: Codex VII, 35, 4 (Feb. 26, 292); IX, 2, 11 (April 6, 292); IX, 9, 25 (Aug. 28, 293).

Sossianus Hierocles   293/305

C. I. L. III, 6661; [Reparato]res orbis sui et Propagatores generis humani DD. nn. Diocletianus ||||||||||| [Invicti]ssimi Impp. et Constantius et Maximianus Nobb. Caess., castra feliciter condiderunt [curam age]nte Sossiano Hieroclete v. p., praes. provinciae, D. N. M.[q.] eorum. (Palmyra).

Although, as far as our information goes, there were senatorial governors of Syria Coele in Diocletian's reign,[48] yet here we find unmistakably an equestrian governor of Syria Phoenice.[49] From the Augusti and Caesares named, the inscription evidently dates between early 293 and 305.[50] Eusebius[51] speaks of a "στρατοπεδάρχης" whom the Romans call dux," at Damascus circa 311/313.[52] It would appear that by that time there was a dux Phoenices. That such an office existed from the very beginning of Diocletian's arrangements is not however thereby proved. Here, in the case of Hierocles, a governor is recorded as building a camp, and no mention of a dux is made. This may then be a slight indication that the governor had command of troops in this period.[53]

Aelius Statutus   293/305

(1) Mél. Fac. Or. (1908), p. 314; (first published in A. J. A. XI (1907), p. 315ff.); Διοκλητιανὸς καὶ Μαξιμιανὸς Σεββ., καὶ Κωνσ-

[48] See under L. Aelius Helvius Dionysius, p. 48.
[49] The V. P. is decisive. C. I. L. III, p. 2463, index, suggests Hierocles as governor of Arabia; but certainly Palmyra belonged to Syria Phoenice. See The Division of Syria, p. 88, and under the next governor, Aelius Statutus, p. 61.
[50] Liebenam, Fasti pp. 118 and 119.
[51] Hist. Eccl. IX, 5, 2.
[52] Schiller II, p. 192ff. Liebenam, Fasti p. 119.
[53] So the governor of Arabia in this period also built fortifications. See Brünnow, Arabia III, p. 294, s. v. Aurelius Asclepiades, and p. 281.

τάντιος κα Μαξιμιανὸς Κέσαρες, λίθον διορίζοντα ἀγροὺ(ς) ἐποικίου
Χρησιμιανοῦ στηριχθῆνε ἐκέλευσαν φροντίδι Ἐλί[ου] Στατούτου τοῦ
δια(σ)ημ(οτάτου).

(2) Mél. Fac. Or. (1908), p. 317; (lines 7-10 reedited by
Littmann in op. cit. (1910), p. 223); Δ[ι]οκλητιανὸς κ[αὶ Μ]αξι-
μιανὸς [Σε]ββ. κ[αὶ ... Κω]νστάντιος καὶ [Μαξιμ]ιανὸς ....
Καίσαρες, [λίθο]ν διορίζιοντα ἄγ[ρου]ς [δημ]ο[σ]ί[ου] Δαρῶν [ἐ]κ
[τῶν τ](α)μιακῶ[ν] Σηοβενας σ[τη]ριχθῆ[ν]ε - - - φρον[τί]δι Ἐλ(ί)ου
[Στ]ατο(ύ)του τοῦ διαση[μοτάτου].

(3) Z. D. P. V. XXXVI, 4 (1913), p. 249; (in part reedited
by Brünnow in op. cit. XXXVII, 2 (1914), p. 151); Διοκλητιανὸς
καὶ Μαξιμιανὸς Σεββ., Κωνστάντιος καὶ Μαξιμιανὸς Καίσαρες - - - φροντίδι Ἐλίου Στατούτου (τοῦ) διασημοτάτου ἡγ(εμόνος).

There are here three inscriptions of an Aelius Statutus
δ ιασημόταος, evidently an equestrian governor.[54] One was
found three or four miles west of Banias, the ancient Caesarea-
Philippi or Paneas (1); another at Djermâna (2), about two
miles southeast of Damascus; the third at il-Kunetra, roughly
twenty-five miles northeast of the Sea of Galilee. As Jalabert,[55] the editor of (1) and (2), says, the date[56] must fall
within the period 293-305. Whether Statutus followed or preceded Hierocles we do not know.

These inscriptions have, I think, some bearing on the question of the province of Augusta Libanensis, formed under
Diocletian, according to the Laterculus Veronensis,[57] and in
the early part of the period 293/305. The assumption that
such a province existed at all under Diocletian rests solely on
the evidence of this laterculus. There is absolutely no other
mention of it. Not even Eusebius, who lived in that part of the
world, in Palestine, during the reigns of Diocletian and Constantine, has a word to say concerning such a province. Damascus, which would naturally fall within its boundaries, is called

[54] As Jalabert points out.
[55] Jalabert's study of the first two of these inscriptions has been accepted by J. Offord in Pal. Explor. Fund (1909), p. 72ff.
[56] The names of the Emperors and Caesars show the date. See
Liebenam, Fasti pp. 118 and 119.
[57] Pub. by Mommsen in K. Akad. Wiss. Berl. (1862), p. 489ff. See
also P.-W. V, 727ff., article by Kornemann; and Brünnow, Arabia III,
pp. 253 and 271.

by Eusebius,[58] a city of Phoenice. Brünnow[59] himself admits that this new province must have soon been reincorporated with Phoenice, certainly at the latest under Constantine.

Now one of these inscriptions is found west of Paneas. This place seems always to have been in the province of Syria Phoenice. Such is the testimony of Eusebius,[60] and of all the authorities,[61] from Ptolemaeus, even before the division of Syria in 194, on through the middle of the sixth century. It is particularly to be noted that, while Damascus falls within the limits of the later province of Libanensis,[62] formed in the last part of the fourth century, Paneas still remained in Syria Phoenice. No one has attempted to show that the early Augusta Libanensis was equal in extent to the later Libanensis, which did not include Paneas.[63] There is every reason then to believe that Paneas was always in the province of Phoenice. Now the inscription (1) comes from that locality, a little west of Paneas. The governor Statutus then was evidently governor of Syria Phoenice. Furthermore, the location of the other inscriptions of this governor, (2) and (3), show that Damascus and the territory around il-Kunetra, southeast of Paneas, also belonged to Syria Phoenice. If then the shadowy Augusta Libanensis ever had an existence, it can only have embraced a very small strip from the extreme southeastern part of Phoenice. In such a case it is difficult to see why the province was termed Libanensis. It must be admitted, of course, that we have no complete evidence, covering the entire reign of Diocletian. But the evidence at hand puts the burden of proof for the existence of an Augusta Libanensis entirely upon those who believe in it, and they have no proof whatever outside the doubtful statement of the Laterculus.

[58] Hist. Eccl. IX, 5, 2 (referring to the period 311/313. See notes 51 and 52) ; Onomasticon, p. 76, of vol. III in Gk. Chr. Schrifst. der erst. 3 Jahrh.

[59] Arabia III, p. 273.

[60] Hist. Eccl. VIII, 15, 17.

[61] See the tables in Brünnow, Arabia III, p. 259ff.

[62] Marq. St. V. I. p. 425.

[63] Emesa, belonging to Phoenice from the time of its formation (Herodian V, 3, 2), and still in that province in Eusebius' time (Hist. Eccl. IX, 6, 1), was placed in the later Libanensis (Marq. St. V. I, p. 425) though it is not much further from the sea coast than Paneas.

GOVERNORS OF SYRIA
BEFORE 70 A.D. (NOTES)

Since the appearance of the third and fourth edition of Schürer G. J. V. (1902), not enough new material has come to light to justify a complete, new study of the governors of Syria before 70 A.D. A few additions to his list (vol. I, p. 302 ff.) may however be noted.

Domitius Calvinus   48/47 B.C.

Schürer[1] thinks that Syria was left to itself for a time after the battle of Pharsalus; but it seems to me very likely that it was among the provinces entrusted to Calvinus.[2]

C. Fonteius Capito   37-35 B.C.

H. A. Grüber[3] shows very reasonably that Capito was governor of Syria when he issued the coins, under Antony, on which he is styled pro. pr., and that this period was 37-35. The lack of any numeral after the Imperatorship of Antony, he explains, is not proof positive that the first Imperatorship alone can be understood.[4]

Pacuvius[5]   22/31

During the time when Aelius Lamia was nominally governor of Syria,[6] a Pacuvius, whom we find mentioned as legate of the Sixth Ferrata at the end of 19 A.D.[7] very probably was

---

[1] G. J. V. I, p. 309.
[2] Bellum Alex. 34, 1 and 3; 38, 2.
[3] N. C. (1904), p. 195 nos. 17 and 18; p. 204.
[4] Münzer, P.-W. VI, 2847, no. 20, on Capito, does not note this work of Grüber at all.
[5] Borghesi V, 92. Liebenam, p. 372.
[6] Schürer, G. J. V. I, p. 329. See Suet., Tib. 41 and 63; Jos., Ant. XVIII, 6, 5.
[7] Tacitus, A. II, 79.

acting governor. Seneca[8] mentions a "Pacuvius qui Suriam usu suam fecit." His position was no doubt similar to that held by Severus during the absence of the governor Publicius Marcellus.[9]

Lucius Popillius Balbus 50

C. I. G. 4529 and 4697b = I. G. R. III, 1209 = 1540 = Milne, Gk. Inscr. p. 14, 33030 ; ἡ βουλὴ καὶ ὁ δῆμος Λούκιον Ποπίλλιον Βάλβον, πρεσβευτὴν Τιβερίου Κλαυδίου Καίσαρος Σεβαστοῦ Γερμανικοῦ, τὸν πάτρωνα τῆς πόλεως.

This inscription is believed to have come originally from Beirût. It is therefore most naturally to be considered as of a governor of Syria. Balbus is, to be sure, simply called legatus ; but the simple form is by no means unparalleled in the early period. Claudius, in whose reign this inscription also falls, is commemorated in an inscription[10] set up by Annius Afrinus, governor of Galatia,[11] who calls himself "leg. eius." P. Sulpicius Quirinus, circa 6 A.D., is called "legatus Caesaris Syriae."[12] Cn. Sentius Saturninus, circa 21 A.D. governor of Syria, is termed "leg. Caesaris Augusti."[13] Ummidius Quadratus, governor of Syria between 50 and 60, in an inscription[14] containing his cursus, is called "legatus - - Neronis Caesaris Aug. in Syria." These inscriptions show that it is quite possible that Balbus was governor of Syria.

The inscription is not definitely dated, but is of the reign of Claudius. Now Petronius was governor, when Claudius became emperor, and was succeeded by Vibius Marsus.[15] He in turn was succeeded by Cassius Longinus.[16] We last hear of Longinus in 49.[17] Then in 51 we first hear of Quadratus in Syria,[18] who continued on into the reign of Nero.[19] For the

[8] Ep. XII, 8.
[9] Governor of Syria circa 132; p. 26.
[10] C. I. L. III, 6799.
[11] Prosop. I, 62, 470.
[12] C. I. L. III, 6687.
[13] C. I. L. III, 6703.
[14] C. I. L. X, 5182.
[15] Jos., Ant. XIX, 6, 4.
[16] Jos., Ant. XX, 1, 1.
[17] Tacitus, A. XII, 11 and 12. Schürer, G. J. V. I, p. 334.
[18] Tacitus, A. XII, 45.
[19] Schürer, G. J. V. I, p. 335.

year 50 then no governor is known, so in that year we may place Balbus. The short duration of his term would account for the failure of Josephus and Tacitus to mention him.

Ummidius Quadratus

Ummidius Quadratus is mentioned as governor of Syria, on a new inscription dated in 56 A.D. A. E. (1907), 194.

UNCERTAIN GOVERNORS OF UNCERTAIN TIME

Syria

I. G. R. III, 1000 (Samosata). Very fragmentary.

[I. G. R. III, 1211] (Gaza). Index (p. 618) lists this inscription as referring to a governor of Syria, without reason.

C. I. L. III, 14387 ee and t. (Baalbek).

VI, 3841.

IX, 3426.

XIII, 2662.

Syria Coele

C. I. L. III, 6823 (Yalowadj).

XI, 599.

Syria Phoenice

C. I. L. III, 185 (Aradus).

III, 125 (Zorava). It is very doubtful if this Theophanes was governor.

Syria

False Inscriptions

* M. Vettius M. f. Sabinianus v. c. C. I. L. VI,[5] 2960. Hopelessly false inscription.

* L. Minicius Fundanus. C. I. L. VI,[5] 3205.

Consul suff. in 107. Proconsul of Asia in 124 or 125.[1] Hence he would be governor of Syria in the period 107/124, if the inscription were good. Unfortunately it has small claim to genuineness.

[1] Prosop. II, 377, 433.

PROCURATORS OF SYRIA

Q. Octavius L. F. C. n. T. pron. Ser. Sagitta
1 B.C./14 A.D.

(1) M. R. I. XXVII (1912), p. 304, 15; Q. Octavius
L. f. C. n. T. pron. Ser. Sagitta, II vir quinq. III, praef.
fab., prae. equi., trib. mil. a populo, procurat. Caesaris Augusti in Vindalicis et Raetis et in Valle Poenina per annos
IIII, et in Hispania provincia per annos X, et in Suria biennium. (Castellvecchio Subequo.)

(2) C. I. L. IX, 3311; Q. Octavio L. f. Sagittae, quinq. II,
pagus Boedinus. (Castelvecchio Subequo.)

(3) Notizie (1898), p. 75; Q. Octavius L. f. S[agitta, quinq.
II?] sacras basilica[s restituendas] et novas facien[das, item
forum?] reficiendum, via[mque ad templum] Romae et Augusti Ca[esaris¹ - - - curavit]. (Castelvecchio Subequo.)

Sagitta was evidently a procurator of Augustus, as the expression "Caesar Augustus" (1) (3), shows. The inscription
(1) is in the ascending order. Now since Raetia and Noricum came under Roman sway by 15 B.C.,² a simple calculation,
based on the number of years in that province and in Spain,
shows that he cannot have been procurator in Syria before
1 B.C. Hence his term falls between 1 B.C. and 14 A.D., the
year of the death of Augustus.³

It is quite possible that Octavius Sagitta, mentioned by
Tacitus,⁴ was a descendant of this Sagitta. If so, the family
had been raised to the senatorial order. We find also mention of a freedman⁵ of the family.

¹ The Notizie does not supply the name, but it seems pretty certain.
² Schiller and Voigt, Röm. Altertümer (ed. 2) in Müller. H. Buch
IV, 2, p. 183.
³ Liebenam, Fasti p. 103.
⁴ A. XIII, 44; H. IV, 44.
⁵ C. I. L. IX, 3035.

(Note on Sagitta, governor in Raetia.) Sagitta is evidently an earlier
procurator-governor than any yet known for Raetia. The conclusion
of M. B. Peaks (Gen. Civ. and Mil. Adm. of Nor. and Raetia, p. 165),

Statilius 18/19

I. G. R. III, 1056, IVa, l. 42ff. (p. 398); - - Γερμανικοῦ Καίσαρος διὰ τῆς πρὸς Στατείλι[ον ἐπισ]τολῆς διασαφήσαντος - - - . (p. 399);
- - quemadmodum etiam Germanicus Caesar in epistola,
scripta ad Statilium, explicuit. (Palmyra).

Statilius was probably a procurator[6] of Syria under Germanicus, hence in 18/19 A.D.[7]

Barbarus 60/63

I. G. R. III, 1056, IVa, l. 56ff. (p. 398); - - ὡς καὶ Κουρβούλων
ὁ κράτιστος ἐσημιώσατο ἐν τῇ πρὸς Βάρβαρον ἐπιστολῇ. (p. 399);
—sicut sanxit egregius Corbulo in epistola quam scripsit ad
Barbarum.

Barbarus was probably procurator[8] of Syria during Corbulo's term, 60-63 A.D.[9]

? C. Plinius Secundus Circa 70

I. G. R. III, 1015; ['Αραδίων] ἡ βουλ[ὴ καὶ ὁ δῆμος . . . .]ίνιον
Σεκοῦν[δον ἔπαρ]χον σπείρης [Θ]ρᾳ[κῶν πρ]ώτης, ἐπαρχον[είλης] . . . .
ων, ἀντεπίτρο[πον Τιβερίο]υ Ἰουλίου Ἀλ[ε]ξ[άνδρου ἐπ]άρχου [τ]οῦ Ἰου-
δαι[κοῦ στρατοῦ, ἐπίτ]ροπον Συρ[ίας, ἔπαρχον ἐν Αἰγύπτ]ῳ λεγεῶνος
ε[ἰκοστῆς δευτέρας].

This inscription, if the opinion of Mommsen[10] is correct,
is of Pliny the Elder. Münzer[11] has doubted this; but Domaszewski[12] accepts it, and shows that the career is quite
normal. The position in Judaea was no doubt held during
the rebellion,[13] so that his procuratorship would be dated
about 70, or soon after.

that Raetia was at first governed by a praefectus (Hirschfeld, Verwaltungsbeamten, p. 390ff.) seems therefore to be incorrect, for the
praefectus cited by her (op. cit. p. 185) is evidently later than Sagitta.

[6] So thinks Hirschfeld, Verwaltungsbeamten p. 90, I.
[7] Prosop. II, 179.
[8] Hirschfeld, Verwaltungsbeamten p. 90, I, also thinks so,
[9] Schürer, G. J. V. I, p. 335.
[10] Hermes XIX (1884), p. 644.
[11] B. J. CIV (1899), p. 103.
[12] Rangord. p. 152. Rh. M. LVIII (1903), p. 225, n. I.
[13] See the cursus of Ti. Julius Alexander, Prosop. II, 164, 92.

67

Aemilius Iuncus Circa 100

B. S. N. A. (1902), p. 341 = A. E. (1903), 116 = R. B. (1905), p. 570; Aemilio [I]unco [p]roc. Aug. (Beirût). Juncus was procurator of Syria at an unknown time. Perhaps he was the father of Aemilius Juncus, consul in 127, as the editors note. The fact that the latter was a citizen and benefactor of Tripolis in Phoenice may increase the probability of relationship.[14] In that case Juncus would be procurator at about the beginning of the second century.

Eudaemon? 117/138

(1) C. I. L. III, 431. (Cf. 7116 and 13674) ; . . . Proc. [Imp.] Caesaris Traiani Hadriani [pro]c. addioecesin Alexandr., [p]roc. bibliothecar. Graec. et Latin., ab epistulis Graec., proc. Lyc. ||| Pamp. Galat. Paph. Pisid. Pont ||, proc. heredit., et proc. pro[vin]ciae Asiae, proc. Syriae. Hermes Aug. lib. adiut. eius. h. c.

(2) I. G. R. III, 1077 = C. I. L. III, 7116; [ἡ βουλὴ κα]ὶ ὁ δῆμος . . . . . . ιμονι, ἐπιτρόπῳ [Αὐτοκράτορος Κ]αίσαρος Τραιανοῦ Ἀδριανοῦ Σεβασ]τοῦ ἐπὶ διοικήσεως ['Αλεξανδρείας ἐπ]ίτροπῳ βι[β]λιοθηκῶ[ν ῥωμαικῶν τε καὶ ἑλ]ληνικῶν, ἐπὶ ἐπιστολῶν ἑλληνικῶν - - - ἐπιτρ[όπῳ Συρίας] - - - . (Beirût).

The man commemorated by these inscriptions was procurator of Syria in Hadrian's reign. From the remainder of the name — ιμονι, (2), Hirschfeld[15] concluded, reasonably enough, that he was the Eudaemon[16] who was high in Hadrian's favor for a time.[17]

Cn. Marcius Rustius Rufinus
Under Commodus?

1) C. I. L. X, 1127; Cn. Ma[rcio] Cn. f. Stel. Rust[io Rufino] praef. class. pr[aet. Misen.], praef. class. Rav[enn., proc.] Aug. prov. Syria[e . . . trib.] coh. I praet., tri[b. coh. XI ur]ban., trib. coh. VI [Vig. - - - - - -.

Rufinus was praef. vigilum 205-207.[18] Before that, but after

[14] I. G. IV,[1] 622.
[15] Friedländer, Sittengesch. I,[6] p. 187.
[16] Vita Hadriani 15, 3.
[17] For treatment of the cursus of these inscriptions see Domaszewski, Rangord. p. 202ff.
[18] E. E. VII, 1204 and 1205. C. I. L. VI, 1056.

198 he was praepositus annonae.[19] This office was apparently an irregular one, for the regular title is praefectus annonae.[20] To this may be due the fact that he is entitled praepositus annonae Imp. L. Septimi Severi Pii Pertinac. et M. Aurelii Antonini Augg. But it is equally possible that the emperors are mentioned because this office was the first one held by him under the new régime. If this is so, then the prefectures of the fleets,[21] and the procuratorship of Syria (1), listed in descending order, must of course be dated before the reign of Severus. This would mean placing the procuratorship of Syria, at least, in the reign of Commodus. It is however possible that Rufinus was procurator of Syria Coele after the division of Syria in 194.[22] A glance at inscription (1) shows that there is space after "Syria[e . . . " which "Coeles" would nicely fill.

Name unknown Probably second C.

C. I. L. III, 183; Fines positi inter Caesarenses ad Libanum et Gigartenos, de vico Sidonior., iussu |||||||||||| pro[c. Aug.] per Dom[itum - - -. (Museiliha).

The procurator's name has been erased. From the general appearance of the inscription we may infer that he probably belonged to the second century.

PROCURATORS FOR PARTICULAR SERVICES IN SYRIA

M. Claudius Q. f. Quir Restitutus Second C.

C. I. L. VIII, 7039; - - proc.[1] - - ad putandas rationes Syriae civitatium.[2]

C. Valerius Quir. Fuscus Second C.

C. I. L. VI, 1633; - - proc.[3] a[d] XX p[e]r Syriam - -.

[19] C. I. L. IX, 1582. The omission of *proc. Syriae* is very curious.
[20] De Ruggiero I, p. 478.
[21] C. I. L. IX, 1582; and (1).
[22] See under The Division of Syria, p. 87ff.
[1] Liebenam, Die Procur. p. 97.
[2] Note that Pactumeus Clemens circa 135 held a position very like this, but as praetorian legate of Hadrian. C. I. L. VIII, 7059.
[3] Liebenam, Die Procur., pp. 63 and 95. Domaszewski, Rangord. p. 162.

PROCURATORS OF SYRIA COELE

? Zosimio 253/260

Vita Claudii 14, 2; Epistola Valeriani ad Zosimionem, procuratorem Syriae. - -

It is not at all certain that there is any history[1] in this section of the Vita; but we note Zosimio as a possibility.

Aelius Ianuarius

Third C., second half.

C. I. L. II, 4135; Ael. Ianuario proc. hereditat[ium], proc. Chosdroe[nes, proc.] Syriae Coeles, [proc.] vect. Illyric[or . . . . .] prov. Hispa[niae Cite]rioris Tarrac[on., prae]sidi prov. Ting[it., praesi]di prov. Mau[ret. Caesariensis . . . . . .

It seems to be the general opinion that Ianuarius was of the time of Diocletian,[2] but there are no real arguments to establish this view or to make it probable. Too little is known of Osrohene, to date the inscription as Liebenam[3] does. So far as concerns the praesides of the African provinces, it is certain[4] that the simple title praeses is found as early as 227 in a cursus inscription; and by 254 in a non-cursus inscription.[5] We may then place Ianuarius in the second half of the third century.[6]

PROCURATORS OF SYRIA PHOENICE

Septimius Vorodes Dec. 262-Apr. 267

I. G. R. III, 1040 ; Σεπτί[μιον Οὐορώδην τὸ]ν κράτιστον ἐπίτροπ[ον Σεβαστοῦ δ]ουκηνάριον, Ἰούλιος Αὐρή[λιος Νεβ]άβαλος Σοάδου τοῦ Αἰ[ρᾶ], στρατηγὸς τῆς λαμπροτάτης κολωνείας [τ]ὸν ἑαυτοῦ φίλον τειμῆς ἕνεκεν, ἔτους δοφ', μηνὶ Ἀπελλαίῳ. (Palmyra).

Cf. nos. 1041-1045 incl., of this same man.

Vorodes was a procurator ducenarius. It would seem that

[1] Peter, Gesch. Litt. röm. Kzeit II, pp. 339 and 340.
[2] Pallu de Lessert, Fastes Prov. Afr. II, p. 353.
[3] Die Procur. pp. 25 and 39.
[4] Pallu de Lessert op. cit. I, p. 507.
[5] Op. cit. I, p. 520.
[6] The name Aelius Ianuarius is quite common; but no other inscription can be assigned to this procurator. C. I. L. III, 1386; 3310; 3347; 12567; VIII, 20425 b; IX, 1410; X, 1742; E. E. VIII, 217; 325; A. E. (1911), 181.

he was procurator of Syria Phoenice; but a "ducenarius"[1] for that province is not likely. Possibly this was given him as title for a special position in Palmyrene affairs, by the Roman government.[2] The inscriptions give the dates Dec. 262 to April 267.

Name Unknown   Third C.?

P. A. E. S. III, A, 655 = I. G. R. III, 1129; - - - - ἐπίτ]ροπον [τοῦ Σ]εβ(αστοῦ), τὸ κοινὸ[ν] ἀγνῶς ἐπι[τά]ξαντα τειμῆ[ς] χάριν. (Aere).

A procurator of Syria, or more probably of Syria Phoenice, since the building in which the inscription was found is dated in 191, is here commemorated. Syria was divided in 194.[3]

Name Unknown   Third C.?

P. A. E. S. III, A, 655[1]; ..... ν .... τὸ κοι[ν(ὸν)] Αἰρη[σ(ίων)] ἐπίτροπον τ[ο]ῦ Σεβ(αστοῦ) τειμῆς χάριν. (Aere).

This inscription, found in the same place as the one preceding, probably also commemorates a procurator of Syria Phoenice.

Antonius Theodorus   Age of Diocletian

I. G. R. I, 1211; Ἀντώνιος Θεόδωρος ὁ διασημ[ότατος] καθολικὸς [τῆς Αἰγύπτου καὶ] Φοινίκης, πολίτης ἐν τῇ βασιλ[ευούσῃ] Ῥώμῃ, χρόνῳ πολλῷ διατρίψας καὶ τὰ ἐκεῖ θαύματ[α] εἶδον καὶ τὰ ἐνταῦθα.

If the restoration of this inscription is correct, Theodorus was a procurator of Syria Phoenice. It is referred, from the term καθολικός to Diocletian's time.[4]

---

[1] On these procurators see Hirschfeld, Verwaltungsbeamten p. 435fl. and Domaszewski, Rangord. p. 149ff.

[2] Sallet, Die Fürsten von Palmyra, p. 11, to which Hirschfeld (*op. cit.* p. 436) refers on Vorodes, I have not been able to consult.

[3] See The Division of Syria, p. 87ff.

[4] Hirschfeld, Verwaltungsbeamten p. 36ff. Daremberg-Saglio IV, 814.

THE SEPARATION OF CILICIA AND SYRIA

After Antiochus had been deposed, in 72, by Paetus the governor of Syria, his kingdom, Commagene, was added to the province of Syria.[1] A large part of Cilicia, especially of Cilicia Trachea, which had been under his sway, was now of course taken away.[2] The problem is to find out what was done with this land. Now the Eastern part, Cilicia Campestris had for long been, and still was, at this time included in the province of Syria.[3] According to Suetonius, Vespasian "Trachiam[4] Ciliciam et Commagenem dicionis regiae usque ad id tempus, in provinciarum formam redegit."[5] The passage unfortunately leaves it doubtful whether new separate provinces were formed or not. Marquardt, however, was inclined to believe from this that Vespasian made Cilicia a separate province.[6] In his second edition[7] on the evidence of an inscription published by Henzen,[8] he put the formation of the province of Cilicia later, under Trajan or Hadrian.[9] This inscription, which gives the cursus of the athlete Flavius Artemidorus[10]

[1] Marq., St. V. I, p. 399.
[2] Ib., note 8; also p. 384ff.
[3] Marq., St. V. I, p. 387. Jos. (B. J. VII, 3, §238) shows pretty clearly, from the fact that Paetus sent troops from Syria to Tarsus to arrest Antiochus, that Eastern Cilicia belonged to Syria. De Ruggiero s. v. Cilicia (p. 231) does not think the deduction necessary.
[4] Reading of M. Ihm's ed. of 1907. Cf. Marq., St. V. I, p. 313, n. 8. Often read "Thracia."
[5] Vesp. 8, 4.
[6] St. V. I¹, p. 229ff.
[7] Op. cit. ed. 2, I, p. 387, n. 10.
[8] Bull. dell Inst. (1887), p. 110 = I. G. R. I, 445. The editors of I. G. R. remark on this inscription: "Nota trium provinciarum legatos, Syriae, Ciliciae, Phoeniciae, in unum concilium eo tempore convenisse." This note seems to me meaningless. Certainly there was no province of Phoenicia at this time, or any legate of it.
[9] So too Kiepert, Atlas (1910) VIII, p. 2.
[10] P.-W. VI, 2533, no. 46.

who had won the first Capitoline games, given by Domitian in 86, mentions a κοινὸν Συρίας Κιλικίας Φοινείκης ἐν 'Αντιοχείᾳ. The assumption made on the basis of this inscription, that Cilicia was still attached to Syria in 86 A.D. has been refuted by Fr. Cumont.[11] He points out that the inscription, evidently put up to celebrate Artemidorus' Capitoline victory, mentions games, in which he had taken part, with little regard for chronological order. Those at Antioch may then have taken place years before. To this we may add from Mommsen,[12] that such games at Antioch might from old custom have been continued after the provinces were politically distinct. Cumont goes on to give more positive proof derived from a new inscription.[13] In it we find a Ti. Iulius Celsus Polemaeanus called "leg. Aug. provinciae Ciliciae," and in Greek form, πρεσβευτὴς Αὐτοκράτορος Καίσαρος Σεβαστοῦ ἐπαρχείας Κιλικίας. Cumont dates the holding of this office of governor of Cilicia before 96 certainly, and probably before 92. On this evidence he goes back, for the formation of the province, to the time when Vespasian took the land from Antiochus.[14] E. Ritterling[15] evidently agrees with Cumont's view.

Recently, however, Domaszewski[16] has asserted that Cilicia remained a part of Syria up to the rule of Trajan, and that the title of Polemaeanus denotes simply a legate of the consular governor of Syria. An inscription of Julius Quadratus, governor of Συρίας, Φοινίκης, Κομμαγένης, Τύρου,[17] before 105, proves of course that by that time Cilicia was no longer part of Syria. Domaszewski, apparently holding the old view of Marquardt, would put the separation as late as possible, hence in the early part of Trajan's reign. One might well be surprised to find such a change taking place during the time when Trajan, after his late return to Rome, was very much occupied with the conquest of Dacia. Further, the interpretation of the office held by Polemaeanus seems to me entirely wrong. In the first place the omission of the "pro pr." in the

[11] Bull. Ac. Roy. Belg.-Lettr. (1905), p. 225ff.
[12] Res Gestae, p. 173, n. 1.
[13] Cumont, op. cit. p. 198. A. E. (1904), 99; (1905), 120.
[14] Op. cit. p. 227.
[15] J. O. A. I. X (1907), p. 306.
[16] Rangord. p. 172, and note 13.
[17] A. E. (1905), 122. Cf. a similar inscription, without Τύρου, in Fränkel, Inschr. von Perg. II, p. 301, no. 437.Cf. above p. 17.

title is by no means necessarily significant. Other cases are found where a governor is certainly meant.[18] In the second place the presence of the word "provincia" with "Cilicia'" is quite decisive. Surely it must mean that the independent province had been formed.[19] Fortunately we have here the help of another inscription,[20] which seems to have been overlooked. It was found at Seleucia, Cilicia, and refers to the building of a bridge διὰ Λ. Ὀκταουίου Μέμορος, πρεσβευτοῖ καὶ ἀντιστρατήγου, ὑπάτου ἀποδεδειγμένου. The date is 77 or 78 A.D. This is the full title of a praetorian governor.[21]

On the evidence of this inscription and that of Polemaeanus, we are surely justified in concluding that, in 77 or 78 A.D., Cilicia existed as an independent province.[22]

[18] C. I. L. III, 6687; Quirinus, circa 6 A.D., is called "legatus Caesaris Syriae." X, 5182; Quadratus, died in 60, "leg. Ti. Caesaris Aug. prov. Lusit., leg. Divi Claudi in Illyrico. eiusdem et Neronis Caesaris Aug. in Syria." C. I. L. VIII, 6706; Q. Lollius Urbicus, "leg. Aug. provinc. Germ. Inferioris" was, no doubt, governor under Hadrian.

[19] A still different view, apparently a compromise between the views of Marquardt and Domaszewski and that of Cumont, is given by Sandys, Comp. to Latin Stud. (1910) p. 403; "Vespasian probably reconstituted Cilicia as a separate province in A.D. 74, consisting of C. Trachea. C. Campestris was added perhaps by Hadrian." That Hadrian added Campestris is a necessary inference from Dig. XXII, 5, 3, 1, where the "provincia Cilicia" is mentioned; with perhaps some consideration of C. I. L. III, 13625, which gives a governor of Cilicia in 121. Evidently Sandys has missed the significance of the inscriptions of Quadratus, to one of which Domaszewski called attention. Moreover, if the view that Trachea was a separate province is held, the inscription mentioned, found in Trachea west of the Lanus (Forbiger, Geogr. II, p. 272) has no proof for the adding of Cilicia Campestris. Then the Digest passage contains the selfsame term which is found in the inscription of Polemaeanus, "provincia Cilicia." So then the main proof, which Sandys apparently uses for the adding of Campestris, may just as well apply to the time of the Flavians.

For the formation of the province Cilicia Trachea by Vespasian, Sandys must have used the passage of Suetonius (note 4 and above) which shows that Cilicia Trachea, if Trachea in the text is correct, was put under provincial government. But Commagene, which was certainly not made an independent province, is mentioned in the same connection, so that it is not possible to conclude that Trachea was then formed as a province distinct from Campestris.

[20] I. G. R. III, 840.

[21] The ὕπατος ἀποδεδειγμένος shows this. Cilicia has always been regarded a praetorian province under the empire. This inscription shows that it was so from the beginning.

[22] See above, and notes 11 and 12.

The territory which this province included, however, may have been Cilicia Trachea alone. That is all that can be inferred from the location of the inscription of Memor. Should Campestris also be included in the new province? I think it should. Now we have shown that the inscription of Artemidorus contains no satisfactory evidence that Cilicia, or any part of it, remained under the jurisdiction of the governor of Syria in the year 86 or later. With the exception of this inscription there is no proof of any kind that Cilicia Campestris remained a part of Syria. If we look at the evidence for its incorporation with Trachea, it is clear that, as has been noted above, no part of Cilicia belonged to Syria in the year 105.[23] Sometime before this therefore, but after 72,[24] Campestris must have been taken from Syria.

Now the new province was under a praetorian governor,[25] but without a legion.[26] There was a number of such provinces in the empire; but I can find no praetorian province so small in extent, with so few important cities, and so insignificant in general, as the province of Cilicia would here have been if it included only Cilicia Trachea. The province of Lycia and Pamphylia, probably the nearest to it in point of size, was considerably larger.[27] Even some of the provinces governed by procurators, Thrace for example, would surely surpass it in importance. It would not be unnatural therefore to expect a procurator for such a province rather than a legate. If, on the other hand, this province included also Campestris, a territory larger and more fertile than Trachea,[28] and having the important city of Tarsus, it would not be at all surprising to find it governed by a praetorian.

Again—an indication is afforded by the political-geographical situation. When Vespasian had deprived Antiochus of his kingdom, there were at least two large tracts of land to arrange under Roman rule, Commagene and Cilicia Trachea.[29] To join both to the province of Syria would be to create a province geographically unwieldy, and perhaps politically dan-

[23] See above, note 17.
[24] See above, p. 72.
[25] See above, and note 21.
[26] Domaszewski, Rangord. p. 173.
[27] Kiepert, Atlas VIII (1910), p. 1.
[28] Forbiger, Geogr. II, p. 272ff.
[29] See p. 72.

gerous. The natural thing to do was to join Commagene to Syria, and this Vespasian did.[30] Trachea, as we have seen, was put under a praetorian governor.[31] Is it not then most reasonable to suppose that, in this readjustment, to balance the addition of Commagene to Syria, Cilicia Campestris was taken from Syria and combined with Trachea, to which it was joined by nature, and by man many years before it came under Roman control? It is quite noticeable also that, with such an arrangement Syria had about the same extent as before, but was much more compact, and could doubtless be better managed.

A further significant fact seems to me to be the founding of a new city Flaviopolis, by Vespasian, in Cilicia Campestris.[32] This fact clearly indicates that changes and rearrangements were being carried on in East Cilicia, as well as in Commagene and Cilicia Trachea. And the time of the founding is especially noteworthy; it was in the year following the deposing of Antiochus, i.e. in 73.[33] Does it not look as if this were part of a general readjustment of Cilician affairs? I think it does. And, I believe, Head was right in his suggestion that the era of Flaviopolis was also the era of the new province of Cilicia.[34] It has been shown that Campestris must have been

[30] See p. 72.
[31] See above, note 21.
[32] Kiepert, Atlas VIII (1910), p. 19.
[33] See note 34.
[34] Hist. Num., index p. 945, s. anno 73-74. The era is given variously as of 73 or 74 A.D. Eckhel III, 56 gives the year 74; Head, op. cit., p. 720, 73 or 74 A.D.; Macdonald, Hunt. Coll. II (1901), p. 533, 74 A.D.; B. M. C. Lycaonia p. CVII, 74 A.D. Imhoof-Blumer, Kleinasiatische Münzen II, p. 445, has collected the evidence for fixing the era, and concludes that it began in 73/74 or 74/75. He doubts the evidence of two coins which, if accepted, would fix the beginning of the era in 73/74. A coin of Antoninus Pius (Babelon, Invent. Wadd. in R. N. (1898) II, p. 165, no. 4286) is dated. ετ. θπ = 89. Imhoof-Blumer considers it a misreading for επ. If correct it gives us, by the era 73/74, 161/162 A.D. Antoninus died on March 7, 161, so the coin would probably have been struck some little time after his death. This is not at all impossible, considering the distance from Rome to Flaviopolis. In Egypt many papyri are found dated, months after an emperor's death, as in his reign (Wilcken, Gk. Ostr. I, p. 800ff). A coin of Elagabalus (Mionnet, Suppl. VII, p. 213, no. 244) dated 149, can only be satisfactorily placed by the use of an era 73/74.

J. H. S. Suppl. II (1892), p. 28, no. 29; p. 21, no. 27 = I. G. R. III, 817 and 818, contains two inscriptions dated by the era of the province.

included in Cilicia before 105.[35] What date is more suitable for this than the time when alone we have evidence for changes not only in Western but also in Eastern Cilicia?

All indications then go to show that the two halves of Cilicia are not to be considered as distinct up to the reign of Trajan, but as parts of one new province formed by Vespasian in 73.

Unfortunately nothing in their content gives us a clue to their dates, so that the era used can not be ascertained.

The year of the rearrangement in Cilicia is taken by Marquardt (St. V. I, p. 384ff.) to be 74, based on Hieron. Chron., sixth year of Vespasian. The statement there given is however only a general summary. Commagene's incorporation with Syria is put under the same year, though, as is certain, its provincial era began in 71/72 (Eckhel III, 253; B. M. C. Galatia—(1899), p. 117). There is in that statement therefore no objection to the placing of the rearrangement earlier, and with the era of the province, in 73.

[35] See notes 17 and 24, and above.

THE REVOLT OF PESCENNIUS NIGER

It has been held by many scholars that the conflict between Severus and Niger was carried on chiefly in 194 and only ended towards the close of that year.[1] G. Hassebrauk[2] expressed the view that the winning of Asia Minor from Niger took place in 193, the final conflict in 194; but he gave no proof. Wilcken's assertion[3] that the revolt was confined to the year 193, I believe can be proved true; but the evidence was not given by him, and his view has not won acceptance. There are however various bits of evidence which demand an explanation of the conflict different from the common one, and which enable us to give a more clearly defined outline of Niger's revolt.

A coin Gabala in Syria is extant, dated in the 240th year of that city, and in the reign of Septimius Severus.[4] Since its era is 47/46 B.C.,[5] it belongs to the year 193/194 A.D. Now it is very likely that the year at Gabala ran from Oct. 1, as at Antioch.[6] Hence Severus was ruler in Syria at the latest, by the end of September 194. The evidence of this coin is supported by coins of Asia Minor. In Galatia, before the end of the provincial year 193/194 A.D., Severus was in power.[7] Coins of Caesarea in Cappadocia give Severus ετ. β.[8]

[1] De Ceuleneer, La Vie de Sept. Sev. (1880), p. 61ff.; especially p. 78. Schiller I, p. 711. K. Fuchs, Gesch. Sept. Sev. (1884), p. 43ff. A. Wirth, Quaest. Sever. (1888), pp. 9 and 24. H. S. Jones, Hist. of Rom. Emp. (1908), p. 240. Domaszewski, G. R. K. (1909), II, p. 252. Liebenam, Fasti (1909), p. 110. R. Cagnat, Epigraphie Latine (1914), p. 208. V. Chapot, Prov. Asie (1904), p. 67, dates it in 195.

[2] Kaiser Sept. Sev. (1890), pp. 12 and 13.
[3] Gk. Ostr. I, p. 803.
[4] Hunt. Coll. III (1905), p. 200, 6.
[5] Eckhel III, 314. P.-W. I, 650.
[6] See under Domitius Dexter, p. 40. B. M. C. Phoenicia p. cxxxix, has Oct. (Nov.) 1.
[7] B. M. C. Galatia—(1899), p. 25, nos. 9 and 14.
[8] Op. cit. p. 73ff., nos. 219, 222, 235.

Since, in all probability, his first year there ran from spring to autumn of 193, his second ran from autumn 193 to autumn 194.[9]

There is also an inscription, a milliarium in Syria, of Venidius Rufus, governor of the new province Syria Phoenice formed under Septimius Severus, and in the year 194 in all probability.[10] It would be very strange to find a governor already repairing roads in 194, if the revolt was not over till near the end of the same year.

Again there is a governor of Arabia, P. Aelius Severianus Maximus, who was in office during the trib. pot. II of Severus, Dec. 193/194, and whose name appears on no less than eight milestones.[11] These call for a date fairly early in 194, at the latest, for the end of Niger's revolt.

A papyrus[12] is extant, dated Sep. 17, 194, which contains mention of Septimius Severus as emperor with the title Arabicus Adiabenicus. These are the titles which Severus took during his campaigns in Mesopotamia, immediately after the suppression of the revolt of Niger. They have formerly been assigned to the year 195.[13] That Severus received these titles at least one month before the date of the papyrus would be a conservative assumption.[14] And moreover some little time must have elapsed, after the end of Niger's revolt, before Severus could have assumed them. A period of three months would be a very small allowance. These considerations alone would fully justify us in placing the end of the revolt and the general course of its events some six or seven months earlier than they are usually dated. To a date as early as the middle of May, 194, objections could hardly be raised.

But we know furthermore, from papyri, that before Feb. 21, 194,[15] Egypt which at first supported Niger,[16] declared for

[9] See note 6, and reference.
[10] See under Venidius Rufus, p. 53, and The Division of Syria, p. 87.
[11] Brünnow, Arabia III, p. 290 for inscriptions. Also C. I. L. III, 14169, 14172, 14174, 14176.[4] See below, note 61.
[12] B. G. U. I, 199, l. 20ff. It is dated in the third year of Severus, month Θώθ κ'. From the Fayum.
[13] Liebenam, Fasti p. 110.
[14] See note 17.
[15] B. G. U. I, 326, col. 2, l.12; Severus emperor.
[16] See below notes 51 and 53. The latest (Grenf. Gk. Pap. II, p. 95, no. 60) is dated Dec. 5, 193.

Severus. Now Wilcken[17] has shown conclusively that a change of emperors was generally unknown for a month and more in central and upper Egypt. It is reasonable then to suppose that Severus was accepted in Egypt as emperor at least a month before Feb. 21. But what good and sufficient reason could there be for Egypt to wish to leave Niger, or even dare·to, when up to the end of 193, according to the usually accepted view, his attempt had been very successful? He had won over all Asia Minor and even held Byzantium.[18] Egypt's acceptance of Severus is only to be understood by supposing that Niger had been killed or at least badly defeated by that time.

Now from another point of attack, namely a study of the acclamations of Severus as imperator during 194 especially, it is possible to date even more exactly the end of the revolt of Niger. It is the generally accepted view that Severus received his second, third, and fourth acclamations during 194.[19] Certain it is that the fourth was the last which occurred in 194, for not only is it found to some extent on documents of 195,[20] but there is also no trace at all of the fifth in 194. Liebenam[21] would date the fourth as late as November, on the evidence of one inscription[22] which gives Severus "Imp. IIII, cos. II, trib. pot. III." This inscription simply shows that Imp. IIII continued in use after Dec. 10, 194. In the light of the evidence from the inscriptions of Severianus Maximus governor of Arabia under Severus trib. pot. II, and Imp. IIII,[23] it contains no proof·that Imp. IIII was not assumed until late in 194. It is plain then that the view that Niger was finally defeated late in 194 has no basis in so far as it rests on the dating of the fourth acclamation.[24]

It has indeed been generally assumed that the final overthrow of Niger must be connected with the fourth acclamation of

[17] Gk. Ostr. I, p. 800ff. His proof is based on the dating of ostraka and papyri.
[18] A. Wirth, op. cit. p. 9.
[19] Liebenam, Fasti p. 109. A. Wirth, op. cit. p. 24.
[20] E.g. C. I. L. VIII, 10351; 10364.
[21] Fasti p. 109.
[22] E. E. VII, p. 425, 5.
[23] See above, note 11.
[24] So Liebenam, Fasti p. 110, apparently dates it. A. Wirth, op. cit. p. 24.

Severus as imperator,[25] though there is no direct proof of this at all, and in fact there is evidence to the contrary. We have seen that Severus assumed the titles Arabicus Adiabenicus for the campaign in Mesopotamia before Sep. 17, 194.[26] The acceptance of such titles would naturally be connected with victories for which an acclamation would likewise be received. The last in 194 with which they can be associated is the fourth. To support this conclusion, which seems a necessary one, there is some direct epigraphical evidence. The titles are found on one inscription[27] of the early part of 195, added after the line "Imp. IIII, Cos. II," and Eckhel[28] refers to another in Muratori's collection. There is also a coin in Cohen,[29] dated in 194 or 195, which reads, "L. Sept. Sev. Pert. Aug. Imp. IIII/Part. Arab. Part. Adiab. Cos. II P. P."[30] The milliarium of Venidius Rufus, first governor of Syria Phoenice, dated in 194 affords evidence leading to the same conclusion. If the "Imp. III" of Severus, on the stone, be the correct reading, as the editor believes, the inscription is in itself absolute proof that Imp. IIII can not be connected with the final overthrow of Niger.[31]

The titles Arabicus Adiabenicus which we have thus connected with Severus Imp. IIII were conferred with this acclamation, and not with the previous one, the third. If they had been given with Imp. III we should rightly expect to see them at least on the military diploma[32] of the city cohorts in 194, and on the inscription set up to Severus by the veterans of the Second Traiana.[33]

We should then naturally turn to the third acclamation as the one to be connected with the overthrow of Niger. That this is the correct conclusion is plainly shown by Roman coins on which Severus is called "Imp. III."[34] Whereas on the coins

[25] De Ceuleneer, op. cit. p. 78; and the references in note 24.
[26] See note 12.
[27] C. I. L. VI, 1026.
[28] VII, 172, ref. to Muratori p. 243, 1.
[29] IV, p. 41, no. 364.
[30] A. Wirth, op. cit. p. 24, without proof rejects this coin, and the inscription (note 27) as false.
[31] See under The Division of Syria, p. 87, and Venidius Rufus, p. 53 (1).
[32] Archaeographo Triestino (1908), p. 289 = A. E. (1908), 146.
[33] C. I. L. III, 6580.
[34] Cohen IV, p. 1ff.

with "Imp. I" and "Imp. II" there are found various expressions of victory such as "Mart. Victo."[35] and "Iovi Vict.,"[36] with "Imp. III" we find for the first time a Peace type,[37] along with other Victory types, plainly indicating that Severus had overcome his rival.

Another bit of evidence for this view is the fact that Severus permitted the regular discharge of veterans of the city cohorts in 194,[38] and more especially the veterans of the II Traiana in Egypt,[39] while he was Imp. III. It seems quite improbable that Severus would muster out troops in Egypt, or even in the city, if he still had a serious revolt on his hands in the East.[40]

We connect then the final defeat of Niger with Severus' third acclamation. The date of this acclamation has been loosely assumed to fall in the middle of 194;[41] but it can now be placed considerably earlier. A military diploma, already referred to, contains mention of Severus as "Imp. III" on January 31, 194.[42] By this date Severus had overcome his rival. This conclusion is not at all out of harmony with the evidence which allowed us to place the end of the revolt at about the middle of May. This date—before Jan. 31—is in fact better suited to that evidence. There is thus a more reasonable length of time allowed between the defeat of Niger

[35] Cohen IV, p. 37, 322, with "Imp. I."

[36] Cohen IV, p. 29, 247, with "Imp. II."

[37] There are two varieties. Cohen IV, p. 35, 308, "Mars Pacator" with "Imp. III"; p. 40, 359, "Paci Augusti" with "Imp. III."

[38] See reference in note 32.

[39] C. I. L. III, 6580; see note 42.

[40] It is of interest to note in connection with the inscriptions of notes 38 and 39, that Liebenam (Fasti p. 110), simply taking a note of Mommsen (St. R. II,³ p. 778, 1) dates the first use of the title *proconsul* by Severus, in 200. Its occurrence however in these inscriptions, with Imp. III and trib. pot. II, shows its use by January 31, 194 (note 42). Cf. also C. I. L. II, 693.

[41] Liebenam, Fasti p. 109.

[42] See notes 32 and 38. The inscription reads: "Imp. Caes. L. Septimus Severus Pertinax Aug., P. P., Pontif. Max., Trib. Pot. II, Imp. III, Cos. II, Procos. — — — a. d. Kal. Febr. Imp. Caes. L. Septimio Severo Pertinax II, D. Clodio Septimio Albino Caes. II, cos." An early date for Imp. III is also made probable by C. I. L. III, 6580, of the veterans of the Second Traiana. Soldiers were "missi" early in January, and finally discharged March 1, according to Mommsen, C. I. L. III, p. 2029. Cf. Daremberg-Saglio III, 1058.

and the assumption of the titles Arabicus Adiabenicus.[43] The fact also that Egypt had submitted to Severus[44] before Feb. 21, 194, is thus best explained—the revolt of Niger was quelled.

The fact that Severus was known as Imp. III by Jan. 31, 194 at Rome makes it practically necessary to set the date of the final victory, for which the acclamation was given, in 193. This victory was won at Issus.[45] In the light of Friedländer's[46] instances of the length of time necessary for journeys in the Roman Empire we are justified in assuming that, at that time of the year, the news could not have reached Rome in less than a month. So then the overthrow of Niger is to be dated near the end of 193 rather than early in 194. That the date must be late in 193 is shown by coins[47] of the second acclamation. They are all of the year 194.[48] This fact clearly indicates that the victory for which the second was taken must have been won late in 193, so late that the news reached Rome only in time to allow the appearance of Imp. II on the early coins of 194.

It is now possible for us to reconstruct the history of Niger's revolt in brief. The revolt began, according to the ancient historians,[49] under Didius Julianus, that is between the end of March and the beginning of June 193.[50] The papyri show that this evidence is substantially correct, since there are a few of the second year of Niger,[51] showing that the revolt must have begun before Aug. 29, 193, which was the Egyptian New Year's day.[52] Furthermore there is a papyrus, from Oxyrhynchus, dated in the first year of Niger, June 14, 193,[53] and there are several others almost as early.[54] Considering the

[43] See above note 12.
[44] See above note 15.
[45] See below note 70.
[46] Sittengesch. I,' p. 306ff.; a journey by boat from Puteoli to Alexandria in nine days; from Rome to Miletus in fourteen days; from Syria to Rome in fifty days.
[47] There are no inscriptions.
[48] Liebenam, Fasti p. 109. Cohen IV, p. 15, nos. 113 and 116; without dates, p. 29, 247, and p. 37, 323.
[49] See Schiller I, p. 671.
[50] Liebenam, Fasti p. 109.
[51] Ox. Pap. IV, 719 and 801. Grenf. Gk. Pap. II, no. 60.
[52] Mitteis-Wilcken I, I, p. liv.
[53] Ox. Pap. IV, 719, l. 28.
[54] Dates of ostraka and papyri, from Niger's first year, are given by

time which must have elapsed before Niger's revolt was known and he was recognized in Egypt, and the long period which usually passed before a change of emperors was known in the inland towns of Egypt,[55] we may safely say that Niger was probably declared emperor in Syria early in April.[56]

All the East was won over by Niger easily and quickly,[57] and yet evidently not all the governors supported his cause enthusiastically. Fabius Cilo, legate of Galatia in 193, left his province, and joined Severus, on the approach of Niger.[58] The governor of Arabia, P. Aelius Severianus Maximus, appointed at least as early as the reign of Pertinax, is found confirmed in his position, in 194, by Severus.[59] Plainly he can have been no ardent adherent of Niger, although no doubt he did not dare to oppose him actively. Perhaps the case of the prefect of Egypt, L. Mantennius Sabinus,[60] is the same; appointed under Pertinax, he appears again early in the reign of Severus, April 21, 194.[61]

Wilcken, Gk. Ostr. I, p. 803; two of June 17, 193; one of July 4; one of July 8.

[55] See above note 17.

[56] Wilcken, l. c.

[57] Schiller I, p. 707ff.

[58] Schiller I, p. 709. Stout, Govs. of Moesia p. 33.

[59] Brünnow, Arabia III, p. 290.

[60] P. Meyer, Hermes XXXII (1897), p. 482. I. G. R. I, 1062.

[61] Domaszewski (Rh. M. LIII (1898), p. 638) argues that the evidence for one and the same governor of Egypt, and also of Arabia, under Pertinax and Septimius Severus, shows that those provinces refused Niger their support, and must have favored Severus from the first. This state of affairs is however only explicable, he claims, on the supposition that the beginning of Severus' revolt is much earlier than usually supposed, is in fact under Commodus. Such an argument throws over not only the literary evidence, but also that derived from papyri and coins, which show beyond doubt that Egypt did favor the party of Niger for at least six months. (See the papyri to which reference is made in notes 51, 54, and 15. For coins, Z. N. II (1875), p. 249.) That Syria Palaestina joined Niger is shown by a coin of Aelia Capitolina (Cohen IV, p. 413, 82). With practically all the Orient thus on his side, it is not reasonable to suppose that Niger set out for Asia Minor, leaving in his rear a hostile province, Arabia. He would surely have attacked it, and subdued it, for its one legion (Domaszewski, Rangord. p. 179) could have done little against his forces.

In this connection there is a papyrus which calls for some explanation. It comes from Nabana near Arsinoe, and is dated in the

The first reverse which the forces of Niger met was near Perinthus.[62] The scene was now shifted to Asia Minor, and again, at Cyzicus Niger's troops, under the leadership of Aemilianus, were defeated.[63] That this defeat, though it resulted in the death of Aemilianus, was not decisive, is shown by the fact that a great battle was later fought in this same region, between Nicaea and Cius.[64] Here Niger himself was so decisively beaten that he was unable to make another stand north of the Taurus range,[65] and thus lost practically all Asia Minor. It was after this great victory, I believe, that Severus received his second acclamation. Since it has been shown that the third is to be referred to the final defeat of Niger, certainly the second can be most suitably assigned to this victory.

Niger then withdrew into Syria, leaving a guard sufficient to hold the Cilician Gates.[66] According to the account of Herodian, the legions of Severus were unable to force the pass for some time, and were becoming discouraged; but finally, after some of the earthworks of Niger's men were destroyed by a heavy fall of snow and rain, the pass was deserted, and the way into Cilicia was open. This whole episode would naturally fall in the winter season of 193/194.[67]

year 1 of Septimius Severus (B. M. Gk. Pap. II, p. 114, no. 351). The date of it, if it is correctly given, must fall before Aug. 29, 193. It has been shown however that Niger was recognized in Egypt by June 14, 193 (note 53). It seems very unlikely therefore that Severus was recognized in Egypt until after the defeat of Niger. I imagine that, after the overthrow of Niger, the year 1 of Severus on this papyrus was intended to date the period before Aug. 29, 194. However, even though Severus was recognized for a short period in 193, the evidence shows conclusively that Niger soon won control in Egypt.

[62] Vita Severi 8, 13; Vita Pesc. Nigri 5, 6. Schiller I, p. 709, thinks that Niger won a minor victory there; but it is doubtful. See Fuchs, op. cit. p. 42. Possibly it was on account of this success of Severus that C. I. L. III, 10398, dated Sep. 11, 193, was set up.

[63] Herodian III, 2, 2. Dio Cassius LXXIV, 6, 4.

[64] Herodian III, 2, 9 and 10. Dio Cassius LXXIV, 6, 4ff.

[65] Herodian III, 2, 10.

[66] L. c. and III, 3, 6.

[67] Note especially Herodian's mention of the snow and rain (Herodian III, 3, 1ff., and III, 3, 6ff.). A. Wirth, op. cit. p. 9, also saw that this episode belonged to the winter, but thought it 194/195, which is not possible. Some scholars have called this part of Herodian a creation of his own fancy (Hassebrauk, op. cit. p. 13, n. 1; and references in Fuchs, op. cit. p. 45, n. 4). Fuchs himself however and Schiller

Meanwhile Niger had been diligently gathering another army,[68] and putting down revolts which had broken out at Laodicea and Tyre, in Syria.[69] At the news that the pass had been taken, he hastily completed his preparations, and advanced to Issus to stay the victorious forces of Severus.[70] There in the final struggle he was again defeated and soon afterwards killed,[71] near the close of 193.[72]

(I, p. 710) accept it as reliable; so too O. Schulz (Von Commodus bis Caracalla (1903) p. 39ff.) who prefers to believe the account of Herodian true, but that of Xiphilinus-Dio, referring the storm to the battle of Issus, false. Dopp (P.-W. VIII, 957) also speaks highly of these portions of Herodian. Whichever view is true it is evident that the last stages of Niger's revolt are to be dated in the winter season.

[68] Herodian III, 3, 6.
[69] Herodian III, 3, 3ff.
[70] Herodian III, 4, 1ff.
[71] Dio Cassius LXXIV, 7 and 8. Herodian III, 4, 2ff.
[72] See above, p. 83. See Appendix, III, p. 94.

THE DIVISION OF SYRIA

Toward the end of the reign of Commodus, Pescennius, Niger had been appointed to the governorship of Syria.[1] Then after the death of Commodus' successor Pertinax, he had made an attempt to gain the empire for himself; but had been defeated and killed by his more fortunate rival Septimius Severus, in the last days of 193.[2] Now it is expressly stated by Herodian[3] that Niger governed the whole of Syria, including Phoenice. An inscription[4] dated in 198, gives Q. Venidius Rufus as governor of Syria Phoenice. It is thus evident that the province of Syria was divided between the years 194 and 198 inclusive.[5]

Jalabert and Mouterde have published an inscription,[6] which they rightly think is of importance for the settling of the exact date when the division was made. This inscription was found near Zahleh, in the territory of Syria Phoenice. It gives Severus "Imp. III,[7] Cos. II," and Venidius Rufus as legatus Augusti. Rufus then is found as governor of Syria Phoenice in 198, and governor, with no mention of province, but in the

---

[1] See above under Pescennius Niger, p. 42.

[2] See under The Revolt of Pescennius Niger, p. 83.

[3] Hist. II, 7, 4.

[4] C. I. L. III, 205 = (3) under Q. Venidius Rufus, p. 53.

[5] Marq. St. V. I, p. 424, very acutely assumed "etwa 194." P. Meyer, Fleck. Jbb. XLIII (1897), p. 594, "about 198." Chapot, Front. Euphrat. p. 164, "vers 198." Brünnow, Arabia III, p. 250, "um 195"; p. 251, "shortly before 198."

[6] Mél. Fac. Or. IV (1910), p. 215ff. = A. E. (1910), 106 = (1) under Q. Venidius Rufus, p. 53.

[7] As the editors note, the inscription may have "Imp. IIII," and it is therefore possible that it dates from early 195. But it probably reads "Imp. III." In either case, since Imp. IIII began before the end of 194 (see the inscriptions in Brünnow, Arabia III, p. 290, under the governor Severianus Maximus in 194, and refs.; also p. 80 above), and since Severus' titles Arab. Adiab. which appear early in 195 with Imp. IIII and V (Cohen V. pp. 40 and 41) are here lacking in an inscription of the East, the date is very probably 194.

territory of Syria Phoenice in 194. The conclusion would seem to be plain, that the province was divided in 194.

There are found however in the lists of Liebenam[8] and Brünnow[9] two governors intervening between Niger and Venidius Rufus, namely Alfenus Senecio and Cornelius Anullinus. Neither of them belongs there. The inscriptions of Senecio are undoubtedly of 198 or later.[10] Jalabert and Mouterde believe that the legateship of Cornelius Anullinus presents considerable difficulty. They are inclined to think that he must have governed between 194 and 198, and that Rufus was therefore twice governor. But there is no proof for Anullinus' governorship at all. The inscription[11] which exhibited him as legate of Syria, is now read[12] with "cur—" in place of "Syr." There is then no reason to believe that Rufus did not govern continuously from 194 to 198.

But now in the new inscription, and in two others[13] of 198 found in Phoenician territory,[14] there is no mention of the province, but only of the governor Rufus. In another inscription,[15] also of 198, the province Syria Phoenice is mentioned. Hence Jalabert and Mouterde[16] conclude that the omission is significant, and that the province was evidently divided some time in 198. Furthermore they think that, since Rufus was consular governor of all Syria, and continued as governor of Syria Phoenice, the government of that province fell to consulars and not to men of the rank of praetor. It is rather unlikely, to say the least, that the consular governor of three legions would be reduced to the command of a small province with one legion.[17] Then too the mere presence or absence of the name of the province after the governor's name seems to me to have little significance. We might as readily argue that

[8] Die Leg. p. 387.
[9] Arabia III, pp. 300 and 321.
[10] On Senecio see above, p. 43.
[11] C. I. L. II, 2073.
[12] C. I. L. II, 5506. See above under P. Cornelius Anullinus, p. 44.
[13] C. I. L. III, 6723; and 6725 = (2) under Q. Venidius Rufus, p. 53.
[14] Marq. St. V. I, p. 423, n. 3, and Brünnow, Arabia III, p. 251, call attention to the fact that the general outlines of Syria Phoenice are given by Ulpian, Dig. L, 15, 1.
[15] C. I. L. III, 205 = (3) under Q. Venidus Rufus, p. 53.
[16] Op. cit. p. 219.
[17] Domaszewski, Rangord. pp. 173 and 179.

a milestone found near Hierapolis,[18] and dated in 197, mentioning neither province nor governor, proves that Syria Coele was separated from Syria Phoenice by that time; for in all the inscriptions of this period on milestones, except this one alone of North Syria, mention is made of the governor Q. Venidius Rufus.

A study of the cursus of Rufus will decide the matter. At a time unknown he was legate of Cilicia,[19] no doubt while of praetorian rank.[20] He is next heard of as legate in Syria, 194-198. In 204 he was curator alvei Tiberis.[21] In 205 he was governor of Germania Inferior.[22]

Now, in the first place, I know of no case where a governor of all Syria later became governor of Germania Inferior. It is always the other way about, and even Britain is held before Syria. After the division Germania Inferior is still held before Syria Coele.[23] This fact is in itself a strong indication that Venidius Rufus was not governor of all Syria.

An examination of the office curator alvei Tiberis makes this certain. The office was usually held soon after the consulship.[24] A study of all the inscriptions, listed by De Ruggiero,[25] extending over a period from Vespasian to Severus Alexander, shows this and a further significant fact. In every case, where a man's complete cursus is given, it is clear that his praetorian governorships were held before his position as curator alvei Tiberis, while his consular governorships were regularly after it.[26] How then could Venidius Rufus hold the governorship of the empire's greatest province some ten years before he was curator? This can not have been the case.

We are now in a position to reconstruct Rufus' cursus. He was praetorian governor of Cilicia. Then he was given a

---

[18] Brit. Sch. Ath. XIV (1908), p. 185.
[19] Dig. L, 6, 3. C. I. L. XIII, 7994.
[20] The province had no legion. See too J. H. S. (1890), p. 251ff., and A. E. (1891), 119; also above, p. 74.
[21] C. I. L. VI, 32332, l. 1; 32327, l. 10.
[22] C. I. L. XIII, 8825; 8828.
[23] Domaszewski, Rangord. p. 180.
[24] C. I. L. VI,[4,2] p. 3109; P.-W. IV, 1790.
[25] Vol. II,[2] 1328.
[26] There are at least ten good cases; C. I. L. II, 6084; 6145; V, 531, 4335, 5262; VI, 1523; X, 3761, 3870; XI, 3364; XIV, 3900, 3902. A. E. (1907), 180. C. I. L. IX, 4194 (uncertain). C. I. L. VI, 1545.

governorship in Syria from 194 to 198. Between 198 and 204 he was consul. In 204 he was curator alvei Tiberis, and in the following year consular legate of Germania Inferior.

It is obvious that, since praetorian governors did not hold Syria, Venidius Rufus could have governed only Syria Phoenice. Hence the division of Syria was made, soon after the defeat of Niger, no doubt early in 194. Septimius Severus doubtless had in mind the fact that two great revolts had taken place under Syrian governors within twenty years, the revolts of Avidius Cassius and Niger. He did not wish to risk a repetition during his reign, and therefore he made an immediate division of the province.

Though Syria Coele[27] remained under a consular, with two legions, IV Scythica and XVI Flavia, Syria Phoenice had only one legion, III Gallica,[28] and was naturally governed by a praetorian. This idea of Domaszewski[29] is now confirmed by our conclusions in regard to the cursus of Venidius Rufus.

[27] Possibly the first epigraphical mention of Syria Coele is found in C. I. L. IX, 1560.
[28] Dio Cassius LV, 23, 2.
[29] Rangord. p. 179.

NOTE ON C. I. L. III, 6169

Stout, Govs. of Moesia p. 55, dates M. Iallius Bassus, governor of Moesia Inferior, in 165 at about the close of the Parthian war; but it seems to me that his connection with Martius Verus, in the inscription, practically proves him governor earlier, that is in the early part of the war. Martius Verus was surely in the East by 165, when Cassius was in chief command (Vita Veri 7, 1. Fronto, ed. Naber p. 131). As leg. V Mac., Verus probably served even in the early stages of the war (Ritterling, Rh. M. LIX (1904), p. 193). It was not furthermore, until the year 166 that Imp. Verus returned from the East (Dodd, N. C. (1911), p. 253. P.-W. III, 1848). Early in that same year Martius Verus was consul suffectus, and thereafter would not be leg. legionis. In fact he seems to have remained in the East as governor of Cappadocia (Liebenam, p. 126. Dodd, N. C. (1911), p. 264).

Now Iallius Bassus was curator operum publicorum Dec. 14, 161 (Stout, Govs. of Moesia, p. 55). In 162 Servilius Maximus was governor of Moesia Inferior. The earliest possible date therefore, for the governorship of Bassus would be the year 162/163, and in that year I would place it.

v. Premerstein, in Klio XIII (1913), p. 89, would have Martius Verus in the East as leg. V Mac. by the year 161/162. The evidence for the date of the governorship of Bassus would indicate, however, that Verus, his subordinate, probably did not go to the East before 163.

INDEX NOMINUM

GOVERNORS OF SYRIA

GOVERNORS OF SYRIA COELE

GOVERNORS OF SYRIA PHOENICE

GOVERNORS OF SYRIA BEFORE 70 A.D. (NOTES)

PROCURATORS OF SYRIA

APPENDIX

I. Waddington (no. 2212, and C. R. Acad. Inscr. N. S. 1 (1865), pp. 120-121) attempted to prove that the revolt of Cassius took place in 172. His argument has been refuted by C. Czwalina, De epistularum actorumque quae a Scriptoribus Hist. Aug. proferuntur, fide atque auctoritate, Bonn. Diss. 1870. See also, Schiller I, p. 658, n. 10; and P.-W. II, 2382. Further proof against Waddington's position is to be found in the fact that, during the very same season in which the revolt was carried on, spring and early summer (p. 36), for the year 172 Marcus Aurelius is known as emperor in Egypt. Fayum no. 207 gives May/June, 172; B. M. Gk. Pap. II, p. 91, early July, 172; B. G. U. III, 769, June/July, 172—all dated by the years of Marcus Aurelius.

Since this thesis has been in press an article by F. G. Kenyon, The Revolt of Avidius Cassius, in Archiv für Pap. Forsch. VI (1913), pp. 213-214, has come to my hand. Kenyon publishes an ostrakon dated in the first year of Gaius Avidius Cassius, June 19. This supplements very nicely the argument drawn from the papyrus (5), p. 33, above. It is chiefly valuable, however, because it states that the fifteenth year, undoubtedly of Marcus Aurelius, was also the first of Cassius. This is proof positive that the revolt is to be assigned to the year 175.

II. In the Sitz. Berl. Ak. (1883), p. 918, no. XVII, Wilcken published a papyrus dated July 25, 175, in the reign of Marcus Aurelius. This evidence makes it necessary to date the revolt still earlier—probably early March to early June.

III. The fact that Niger's revolt was suppressed at the end of 193 makes it necessary to place the beginning of the siege of Byzantium in the summer of 193. Since it is generally agreed that the city fell in 196 there is no adequate reason for doubting the accuracy of Dio's statement, as A. Wirth (Quaest. Sev. p. 28) and Kubitschek (P.-W. III, 1139) have done, that the siege continued for three whole years. (See Dio Cassius LXXIV, 12, 1).

www.ingramcontent.com/pod-product-compliance
Lightning Source LLC
Chambersburg PA
CBHW060423090426

42734CB00011B/2425